YOU LITTLE JERK

HOW TO CREATE CULTURE AT HOME, AT WORK, AND EVERYWHERE ELSE IN YOUR LIFE

Larry Hubatka

BISMARCK
SQUINCEE

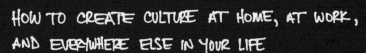

ISBN 978-0-9998302-1-5

Design: Larry Hubatka, Scott "Cheddars" Brinkley, Lucy Hubatka
Line Editor: Julia Pastore
Copy Editor: Christy Bock, Signe Jorgenson, J2
Lead Encourager: Kelly Hubatka

Books are available at a discount when purchased in bulk or for
educational use. Special editions may be printed upon request. For
more information, please contact *hello@youlittlejerk.com*.

Printed in the United States of America

First printing Dec 2019

youlittlejerk.com

To PSF

Thank you for inviting me
to share Pantone 165 with the world.

Table of Contents

Part 1: UNDERSTANDING CULTURE

Part 2: CREATING CULTURE

FOREWORD

WRITTEN BY THE JANITOR FROM MY OLD JOB

I used to clean a church building in Charlotte, North Carolina, a few times a week, and I always wondered what I'd be walking into whenever I showed up. Typically, I worked in the middle of the night, and it was just supposed to be two or three of us from my team. It rarely turned out that way.

Every time I walked into the building, the music was loud and several people were still hanging around. It wouldn't be long before someone would come rolling through the lobby on a scooter, a bike, a trash can, a wheelbarrow, or one of those old sit-down things that you wiggle back-and-forth to make it go.

To be honest, I had no idea what they were doing there most of the time. They were just a bunch of kids running around in the middle of the night doing God knows what.

One time, I saw someone putting hundreds of sticky notes all over the wall. Later in the week, I noticed they had become someone's giant face—a mosaic made out of sticky notes! Another time, I ended up in a video for an awards show the kids were hosting. Right place, right time, I guess. I was glad to help.

Over the years, I saw a lot at that church office in the middle of the night. I don't know how it all worked over there, but I do know they enjoyed themselves. It was something special.

And, when it was all said and done, they even threw me a retirement party before I left. Those kids were okay, I guess . . . when those jerks weren't making a huge mess, getting in my way, and slowing me down in the middle of the night.

Ric
Former Night Shift Janitor

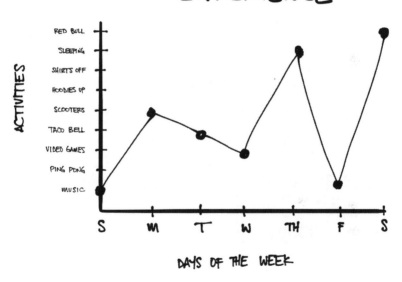

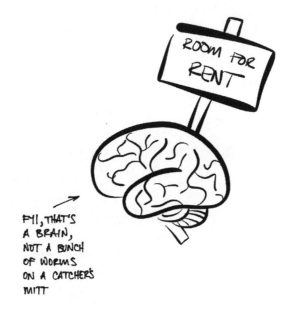

PREFACE

I find it interesting to study how people change their minds. What really happens inside someone's head? It seems to flow like this:

First, you form an initial opinion based on your understanding of the subject matter. Then, you become more informed. (Maybe through social media, friends, books, conversations, events, gossip, eavesdropping, the back of a cereal box, whatever.) This new insight influences your perspective, and your opinion evolves as a result.

What's especially interesting is that changing our minds is often portrayed as negative. Many people resist change altogether. I find it to be one of life's greatest freedoms — the fact that you can become educated to the point of new understanding and better decision-making.

As this book was coming together, my research and notes looked a lot like a collection of everyone else's opinions and perspectives at first. They were a compilation of concepts that moved me, quotes that compelled me, and principles I found inspiring. Everything was sourced from many of my favorite people—authors, coaches, pastors, and friends. Collectively, these insights and opinions from others challenged my take on culture and how it's formed. They eventually led me to develop a fresh point of view on the matter.

There are countless options for how to influence culture. However, over the last 20 years, I've discovered several common threads between the various organizations, environments, and cultures I've researched or personally experienced. I encourage you to read and process these discoveries along with my own interpretations, insights, and stories. Then, allow them to inform *your* opinion and maybe even influence what you believe about creating culture—not which cultures are better or worse, but rather your capability of building one that's right for you.

* OFTEN WITH A
NEW PERSPECTIVE

GOT IT

PART 1

UNDERSTANDING CULTURE

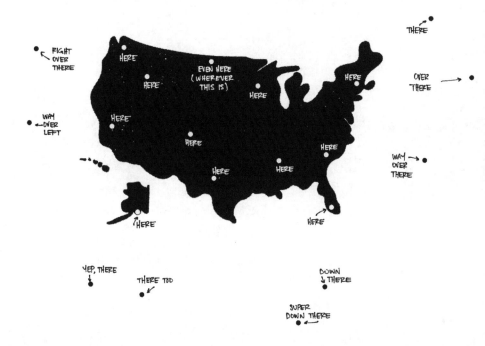

WHY I WROTE THIS BOOK

"Look what ya did, you little jerk."

That line from *Home Alone*—coupled with the uncle's facial expression—is unforgettable. I don't know if it's because I can't stop visualizing the old guy's disparaging face when he says it or if it's because I feel bad for Kev. Either way, when Chris Columbus (yes, that's actually his name) directed *Home Alone* in 1990, he delivered enough punch in three seconds to keep that phrase top-of-mind for thousands of people around the world ever since.

Specifically, there are two reasons I love it:

First, *Home Alone* is synonymous with Christmas. It plays about 175 times during the Christmas season on TBS and TNT, and I've watched at least part of it every year since it was released. In the classic movie category, that kind of syndication gives it Hall of Fame status — *Shawshank Redemption, The Devil Wears Prada,* and *Twilight.* It's part of our Christmas culture, and we keep passing along that culture to the next generation. Ask 15-year-olds today. Even they know the line, and they weren't even close to being born when the movie was released!

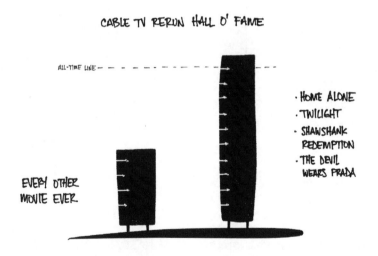

CABLE TV RERUN HALL O' FAME

ALL-TIME LINE

EVERY OTHER MOVIE EVER

- HOME ALONE
- TWILIGHT
- SHAWSHANK REDEMPTION
- THE DEVIL WEARS PRADA

Second—and more interesting to me—is how that single line highlights one of the biggest secrets about culture: jerks. I'm guessing Chris Columbus didn't do it intentionally, but you never know. If you have "Directed *Home Alone*" and "Discovered America" on your résumé, you're clearly operating on another level. Maybe it *was* on purpose.

Look at the last word in the quote: "jerk." In this instance, it's the kind of "jerk" that describes your neighbor who can't remember to pick up his dog's poop in your yard—again. Bro, ever heard of Ring? We can all see that it's you! There's also the kind of "jerk" that describes the Jamaican chicken my wife and I get from one of our favorite little restaurants when we're on vacation at the beach. And then, there's the kind of "jerk" as in "knee jerk," the reflex response when the doctor uses the little triangle-shaped hammer on your knee. This last one is the "jerk" I want to talk about because jerks and culture are more connected than you realize.

"Knee jerk" is a culture word.

This is how we describe an involuntary reflex—a knee-jerk reaction—and this is exactly what culture does. Culture creates reflexes that prompt us to respond without thinking. A major part of recognizing culture is observing reflexes. When culture is strong, you won't have to voluntarily think or act a certain way all the time. Like associating *Home Alone* with Christmas, it's automatic. A reflex. There's a reason it feels wrong to watch *Home Alone* in July . . . unless you live in Australia, mate. (But, I draw the line at Summer Santa wearing a tank top; that's weird for us in America. It would be like seeing your dad in a Speedo. You just don't like the thought of it.)

For instance:

- If the culture of your home is welcoming, you offer guests a drink when they come inside without even thinking about it.
- If the culture around your office is to present the organization professionally, employees will pick up a piece of trash on the ground without being asked to do so.
- If the culture of your sports team is winning, teammates will

put in extra work after practice without being asked.

Our reflexes are the strongest indicator of our culture.

These are not just behaviors, but reflexes. Behaviors and reflexes often look similar. However, behaviors can be manufactured while reflexes can't be helped—they're automatic. Pay attention to the natural reflexes of the people around you and you'll discover what kind of culture you have.

I wrote this book to help you discover how to build a better culture; how to create a new set of reflexes that reflect the behaviors, beliefs,

YEP, LOOKS LIKE
WE'VE GOT CULTURE

and values you want at home, at work, and everywhere else in your life. Of course, you probably won't see a radical transformation overnight, but you will begin to see small, encouraging signs of change rather quickly. There won't be a huge knee jerk right away, though, because lasting change takes time.

But, imagine the moment when you realize real change is coming because you notice that small, sudden reflex one day. That barely noticeable, involuntary movement. That little jerk. That's the moment that "look what ya did, *you* little jerk" becomes "look what ya did: *a* little jerk." The tone of that statement changes entirely from condemnation to hope.

It'll be an epiphany, an indication that the effort you put in is finally coming back to you. You will have fostered a culture change. A little "jerk" is the first sign that you're on the right track to building the culture you've been hoping for.

Congratulations. You're officially a *Jerk*.

LOOK WHAT YA DID...

1990

COMING SOON

...YOU LITTLE JERK

...A LITTLE JERK

EPIPHANY REQUIRED

HOW TO USE THIS BOOK

This book is an introduction to culture. It won't solve all of your problems, but it will provide context and get you started down the right path.

I wanted this book to be simple and short, something you could read in a couple of hours. If you make it a bathroom reader, that's fine. (Just try not to lead with that if we ever meet.)

I don't consider myself an expert at much of anything, but I'm pretty good at talking and doodling. This book is a collection of talking (I dictated about 90% of it in my car) and doodling; you're getting a picture of how my brain works. I wanted lots of visuals to help make the content memorable, so this book is full of doodles, sketches, charts, and illustrations.

More than anything, I wanted this book to be helpful.

Culture is transferable. This book is full of research- and experience-informed thoughts on culture that are designed to be easily understood and shared on a napkin so you can pass them along. It's full of stories because stories are how I've always learned best. They're what I remember most from the books I read. I believe creating a frame of reference is the fastest way to learn, and stories help do that more than anything else.

STORIES = I GET IT

STORIES PROVIDE SUPPORT BY GIVING US A
FRAME OF REFERENCE. LIKE A LANDMARK
HELPING US GET FROM ONE PLACE TO THE NEXT

When I had the idea to put this book together, I pictured sitting down with someone and scribbling out a few illustrations. At the risk of sounding pretentious for treating you like a remedial art student, I really dumbed it down and made many of the illustrations easily replicable for doodlers of all levels. This means that, in some instances, I'm giving you a diagram for exactly how I'd sketch out the idea and what I might say if I were passing it along. Of course, take my notes and deliver them however you'd like. You don't work for me. You're the boss in this book, and this book works for you.

It's not a set of guidelines written to judge whether or not you're doing a good job; it's a tool to help you become a culture-maker. Use it however you'd like. Read it in one sitting, or when you have a few minutes, or as needed. This book is a tool intended to make your life better, not something to hold you back. And, if it turns out to be terrible, at least it's a 6x6" square. That way, you can tear out pages and frame them; it'll be all Instagrammy and super artsy. People will think you're so on-trend. It's a win-win.

10 INSTAGRAM IDEAS

FOR WHEN YOU'RE OUT OF IDEAS OR JUST WANT
TO FOLLOW WHAT EVERYONE ELSE DOES

1. YOUR OUTFIT
2. FLATLAY WHAT'S IN YOUR BAG
3. BEHIND-THE-SCENES
4. ASK A QUESTION
5. BOOK RECOMMENDATION
6. SCRIPTURE & SELFIE   #HUMBLEBRAG
7. LOTS OF WHITE SPACE
8. DIY PROJECTS
9. YOUR COFFEE
10. EVERYONE LOVES A DOG POST

COLLEGE
CULTURE

WHAT IS "CULTURE?"

Culture is how I slept on a futon all throughout college without ever changing my sheets. It's how your daughter lays on her bed binging *Gilmore Girls* at 3 p.m. on a sunny Saturday afternoon. It's how you tell your boss you need help without fear of humiliation or shame. (Or, how you *don't* tell your boss you need help due to fear of humiliation or shame.)

Culture is your way of life:

- It's how you live, what you believe, and the values that guide your day-to-day experiences.
- It's bigger than you.
- It defies logic.
- It seems to sustain momentum for a while. And, eventually, it loses steam if you're not intentional about it.

- It's strongest when reinforced.
- It can be manufactured.
- It can be good or bad.
- It works better when trust and vulnerability are present.
- It's contagious; it spreads faster when gratitude is involved.

You know you want it, and you're not quite sure when you've built it. Silicon Valley and disruptive tech companies have made it popular. It's bigger than a business buzzword. When it's good, it's great. When it's unhealthy, it's debilitating.

This is culture.

Here's the working definition we'll use throughout the book:

Culture is the collection of behaviors, beliefs, and values we generally accept and transfer to others without consideration.

BEHAVIORS BELIEFS & VALUES

(IT'S LIKE A BLT, BUT SUB B FOR L AND V FOR T)

Culture is the collection of behaviors, beliefs, and values . . .
Note that it's a *collection* of behaviors, beliefs, and values. (By the
way, I'll be referencing "behaviors, beliefs, and values" a lot, so
whenever you see "BBV," that's what we're talking about.) This
implies there's more than one of us involved and more than one
behavior, belief, or value to consider. Multiple people are required to
create any culture. If it's just one person, it's less of a culture and more
of an idea, personality, or habit. People are what bring culture to life.
You can have a strong personality, but that doesn't automatically result
in a strong culture. Do effective leaders with big personalities often set

the tone for a culture? They sure do. A big personality is not required, but it will expedite and heavily influence whatever culture is being established.

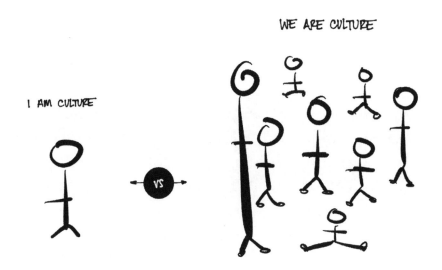

... *we generally accept* ...

We have to *accept* these behaviors, beliefs, and values for them to become culture. I've heard it said, "We accept what we allow." When it comes to culture, our *acceptance* often takes the form of *allowance*. When we take no stand or have no opinion, unfortunately, we are absolutely taking a stand and expressing an opinion.

Acceptance is a requirement for culture—whether we agree or not.

It's possible to live in a culture we dislike. But, if we don't do anything about it, it remains a way of life. For example, your office culture may be toxic because people regularly say negative things about co-workers behind their backs. Unless you decide to take action and address the issue, this is the culture you're stuck with.

There's a difference between *agreeing* and *accepting*. For example, when you "agree to disagree" in an argument, you're accepting the other person's position, but not agreeing with it. Similarly, you may very well agree to disagree when it comes to culture in your home or

JUST BECAUSE
YOU DON'T LIKE
IT DOESN'T
MEAN IT'S NOT
PART OF THE
CULTURE

workplace, but it's still a form of acceptance.

... and transfer to others ...

Culture is transferable. If it requires a group of people to sustain it, then the individual behaviors, beliefs, and values associated with the group are like the DNA of the culture itself. We pass those "building blocks" along to others through shared experiences, conversation, and proximity. For example, when I saw *The Greatest Showman* musical for the first time, I couldn't stop talking about it. I had the soundtrack playing for six weeks straight! And, if we spent any time together during those few months, the more we were together, the more likely it was that my obsession rubbed off on you a little bit. If you were anywhere near me between February and April 2018, I'm sorry you had to endure that, but . . . "This Is Me."

Every persuasive conversation moves us, even slightly, in some direction. The sheer volume of conversations around any single topic will eventually have an effect on us. If I talk to you about the Seattle Seahawks and the Washington Huskies every day (and I probably will), you'll come to realize that I've got some unhealthy Seattle-football-groupie tendencies about me . . . and I just might begin to influence your perspective over time as well. However, my tendencies, while transferable, don't become culture until others around me begin to accept them, even passively. In the meantime, they're simply a part of my overly extreme personality.

This is how proximity influences culture. It's why your parents told you, "Bad company corrupts good character." It's also the reason why you ought to be mindful about taking advice from your buddy Grant too often; he's the guy who misspelled "fredom" on his DIY forearm tattoo. I'm not encouraging you to live life judging whether people are good enough for you. I'm only saying you should be mindful of who you allow to influence you by proximity because they'll eventually transfer some of their behaviors, beliefs, or values to you.

... *without consideration.*

We've got to be intentional to create and sustain the best cultures, but the truest validation is when our behavior becomes automatic. Remember the little jerk, that reflex? That will tell you as much as anything about the strength of the culture you live in. It'll also validate that a particular way of life does exist. When you get up and work out every morning without having to shame yourself into it, or when your kids voluntarily say, "Thanks, Mom" after you make them dinner, there's something beginning to bud there.

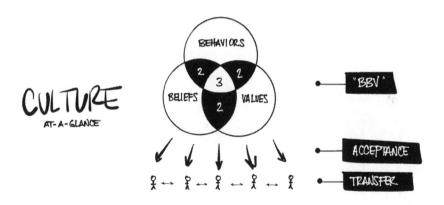

I should mention that we can look the part without having authentic motivation. Your kids can say "thank you" or "sorry" to a sibling without meaning it because they just don't want to listen to you talk at them for the next 10 minutes. They're smart. Their behavior may not be the purest, healthiest example of the culture you want, but recognize that it's a start and a confirmation that they're capable of eventually developing sincere reflexes.

There you have it, the framework that will guide us through this process of building a better culture. Our awareness of the elements that create culture gives us a starting point. And, if you take one thought away from this book, here's my recommendation:

You're always creating a culture, so create the one you want.

WHAT DO YOU WANT?

(I WANNA REALLY REALLY REALLY WANNA ZIGAZIG AH)

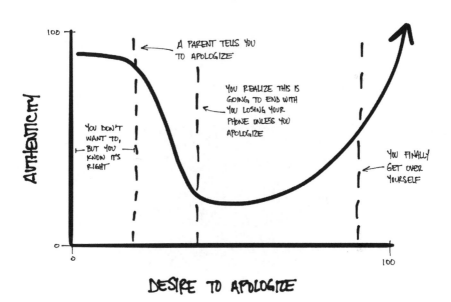

KIDS AND APOLOGIES
UNDERSTANDING FORCED APOLOGIES

AUTHENTICITY (y-axis, 0 to 100)

DESIRE TO APOLOGIZE (x-axis, 0 to 100)

YOU DON'T WANT TO, BUT YOU KNOW IT'S RIGHT

A PARENT TELLS YOU TO APOLOGIZE

YOU REALIZE THIS IS GOING TO END WITH YOU LOSING YOUR PHONE UNLESS YOU APOLOGIZE

YOU FINALLY GET OVER YOURSELF

FRESH BAKED CULTURE

REVIEWS: 4.8/5.0   **PREP TIME:** 30-365 DAYS

1 GROUP OF PEOPLE
1 MOTIVATED LEADER
6 WORK ETHICS
12 DO-OVERS
250 PATIENCE

How can I actually create culture?

Out of frustration, everyone I know has uttered some version of this statement to a friend, spouse, or significant other: "Just tell me what to do, and I'll do it."

Unfortunately, this is a relational tension that will never be resolved. However, culture is one area that actually *can* be affected with a just-tell-me-what-to-do approach. While relationships aren't likely to ever follow much of a template, building a better culture does. Here's the framework:

Create consistent experiences that reinforce behaviors, beliefs, and values, and connect them to emotion.

CREATE
CONSISTENT EXPERIENCES

+

REINFORCE
BEHAVIORS, BELIEFS, & VALUES

+

CONNECT
THEM TO EMOTION

CULTURE FRAMEWORK

This is the secret to creating culture. No one talks about this because it doesn't seem realistic to explain something as nebulous as culture this easily, right?

Go back and study the most prolific corporate cultures of our time— Starbucks, Apple, Zappos, Disney, the Seattle Seahawks from 2012-2019 (I warned you). You'll find this framework as a common thread. The more consistency, the more pronounced the BBV (behaviors, beliefs, and values), the more emotionally charged the environment; the stronger the culture.

Create consistent experiences...

Anyone can reinforce BBV and connect it to emotion once or twice, but can you *consistently* do this in a manner that becomes natural and intuitive? That's the magic question. Your answer will determine whether the culture you're developing will last and thrive, or if it's just a moment you manufactured for a minute. This is the difference between a culture and a one-off or short-lived experience—the lasting influence on BBV through consistency.

Think of it this way: The most successful organizations, teams, and individuals you know are the ones that figured out how to operate consistently on a daily basis. We're all capable of peaking now and again, but can we do it regularly? Anyone can post a viral video on accident every once in a while. The real content pros are able to do it over and over and over again.

... that reinforce behaviors, beliefs, and values ...

BBV is the reason people love culture. Imagine an environment at home or at work where people generally do the right things, say the right things, and believe the right things—whatever those are for you.

If you told me there was a realistic way to align people around behaviors, beliefs, and values, my first question would be, "How do I do that?" It's almost unbelievable to think it's possible, and this is the allure of having a desirable culture.

In my research, the most common statement I heard when interviewing individuals who enjoyed their work environments was some form of "I love the culture." Most people don't actually know what they're saying when they say that. But, they know what they mean—"I love the BBV all around me. I love the way of life all around me."

Culture is influenced by BBV, and it helps sustain BBV as you continue growing. Typically, you can't use a word to define itself (e.g., happy ≠ when you're happy). But, this is exactly what happens with culture—BBV is culture, and BBV creates culture. It defies logic. This is one of the many reasons people are so obsessed with building a great culture.

: WARNING :

A CULTURE YOU LOVE

ATTRACTS PEOPLE YOU LOVE

THEY STRENGTHEN THE CULTURE YOU LOVE

YOU'RE SO HAPPY YOU DECIDE TO GET A DOG

... and connect them to emotion.

Remember when I mentioned in the last chapter that a leader's strong personality is not necessary for creating culture? Although it's true, here's the reason that the two—namely, a strong personality and an established culture—are often connected. The secret sauce is in the emotion evoked by that leader.

Emotion is the glue that makes everything in your culture stick.

GLUE
IT'S FOR MORE
THAN JUST EATING

In the 1970s, a Harvard study called the Flashbulb Memories determined that people are often able to vividly recall where they were when they learned of a significant event. At the time, the researchers used the assassination of President JFK as the example. But, consider a personal example of your own:

- Where were you when you heard the news of 9/11 in 2001?
- What was the word you missed when you were eliminated from the fourth-grade spelling bee?
- What were you doing when you discovered you were in labor with your first child?
- What was happening when you got the news that your parents were getting divorced?

We remember interesting details about moments and experiences—both positive and negative—that emotionally move something within us. Most psychologists agree that the connection between emotion and recall is real, but researchers still don't have a sound explanation for why.

THAT GUY WITH THE BIG TEETH GOT ME GOOD

Prolific leaders are often some of the best culture builders for a reason: They're exceptional at making you feel something. When emotion wells up within you—even for a minute—it's like a Venus flytrap opening up. Whatever hits the trap is about to be captured by the sticky tentacles and ingested. That's exactly what happens internally when our emotions are activated.

Whether we're describing Tony Robbins, Ellen, or your favorite high school teacher, they all possess the same superpower: They're good at making you feel something. Interestingly, lots of people have the ability to make you feel something—big personalities, comedians, bullies. So, what sets the culture builders apart? They know what to do with the emotion once they create it. They feed the right BBV to that

Venus flytrap when it's open.

Tony Robbins is a self-help/motivational legend. When I first saw a picture of him, I thought, "Hey, that's the guy with the big teeth. I see him everywhere!" He's a large man with pronounced features, and he has a presence about him.

I sat through a Tony Robbins workshop years ago for professional development. It was an event I attended with everyone from the office

ALL THE FEELS
WHY ARE SOME PEOPLE GOOD
AT MAKING US FEEL?

TONY ROBBINS   ELLEN   YOUR HS TEACHER

at my first job out of college. I really didn't think I'd get much out of it. I assumed he was a little kooky (because I chronically judge books by their covers). But, something unexpected happened to me that morning: I discovered why he's so mesmerizing. I sat through a session and, by the end of it, I was up on my feet, rocking back and forth, pounding my chest, and screaming at the top of my lungs in a room with 18,000 other people. Running through my head at that moment was, "Look at me, I'm incredible! I am sooooo rad!"

Needless to say, I was amped. Tony had done his job. Again. Like he does every time he speaks at any event. There's a reason he can justify a $10,000 price tag for attending some of his events.

I remember sitting in the upper deck of the Rose Garden in Portland, Oregon, like it was yesterday — and this happened in 1999! Our recall of details from personal, high-emotion experiences is extremely strong. Emotion is the glue. And, Tony Robbins is clearly some kind of feelings wizard.

MEMORIES

SELECT MEMORIES I CAN CLEARLY
RECALL THAT ARE AT LEAST 30+ YEARS OLD

GETTING IN TROUBLE
FOR COMING HOME
LATE FOR THE FIRST
TIME... 6 YEARS OLD

GOT IN THE MOST TROUBLE I
HAD EVER BEEN IN.

HITTING A HOMERUN
IN LITTLE LEAGUE...
10 YEARS OLD

I'D NEVER DONE IT BEFORE.
I DIDN'T THINK I COULD.

GOING TO MY BEST
FRIEND'S HOUSE AND
BEING OFFERED
GATORADE... 12 YEARS OLD

I NEVER GOT TO HAVE GATORADE.
IT WAS TOO EXPENSIVE GROWING UP.

COMMON THREAD?

THEY WERE ALL PERSONAL,
HIGH-EMOTION EXPERIENCES

Tony's intentional ability to create an experience (the event itself) that reinforced behaviors, beliefs, and values (the belief that I am capable) and connect them to emotion (I felt invincible in the moment) left me energized. Perhaps you believe my personal experience with Tony—or similar experiences—are nothing more than hype. But, this book is written with an assumption in mind:

Humans are designed to respond to certain dynamics and stimuli. We're not robots, but there is a natural order to how we respond. We respond to emotion, whether we choose to express it or not. We're influenced by what we're immersed in. Our experiences radically affect who we are and how we live.

While there are varying degrees to how every individual responds to emotion, the principle that emotion influences BBV is true nonetheless.

Ultimately, you don't have to believe cycling is an effective form of exercise to ride a bike. It'll get you from your house to Trader Joe's for that crunchy almond butter whether you believe it's effective exercise or not. Along the same lines, you don't have to believe there's a framework for building culture, either. It's just that everyone who embraces this framework is enjoying the benefits of a stronger, more enjoyable culture. And, they're probably living it up with a dozen almond-butter-banana-honey sandwiches right now while they watch another *Shawshank Redemption* marathon on TBS.

CULTURE'S INGREDIENTS

EXAMPLES

Create consistent experiences...
Monthly happy hour with the team from your office

...that reinforce behaviors, beliefs, and values...
We place a premium on personal relationships

...and connect them to emotion.
Pay for a round of drinks and watch everyone smile

EXAMPLES

Create consistent experiences...
High point/low point dinner conversation with the kids

...that reinforce behaviors, beliefs, and values...
We prioritize intentional communication as a family

...and connect them to emotion.
Create feelings of acceptance by affirming your kids for sharing openly

EXAMPLES

Create consistent experiences...
Weekly book club with friends

...that reinforce behaviors, beliefs, and values...
We discuss how the weekly reading has affected us personally

...and connect them to emotion.
Everyone experiences emotion (joy, insecurity, etc.) from being in the spotlight and sharing their responses

PART 2

CREATING CULTURE

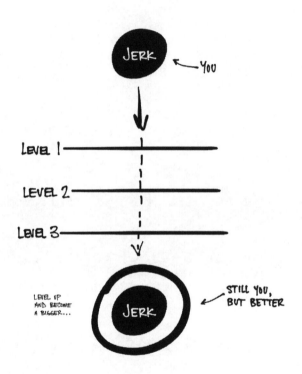

SKIP AD

In this section of the book, I've provided 30 thoughts on how to create culture. It's a collection of anecdotes to help you wrap your mind around the practical side of this process—how to apply various tactics to our culture framework. While this section is intended to help expand your scope regarding the tools you'll need, the processes you'll implement, and the perspective you'll use to filter your decisions, it's more of an introduction than it is a prescription.

If you find yourself wanting to expand beyond the basics of creating culture discussed in this book, your next steps will be to walk through the blueprint process of building your custom culture. You can do so by going through the *You Little Jerk Workbook* or by visiting culturepants.com for tools, resources, and workshops that will help bring your culture to life.

1

WHY I APPRECIATE FAT THIGHS

IDENTIFY YOUR STARTING LINE

I have a friend named Buck whom I've labeled with a "Top 3 Physically Fit Friends" label. (I've labeled lots of my friends . . . fastest response time, sweatiest, vacation blacklist, etc.). Buck is the kind of fit that passes the firefighter fitness test on the first attempt.

One afternoon, after taking a little break from working out—and by "little break," I mean I hadn't worked out at all for about six months—I was at a boot camp workout he was running. (I had success with high school sports, so, naturally, I have a delusional optimism about my athleticism in my 40s.) This particular workout included 10 different exercises, and we were doing 50 reps of each exercise. Do the math . . . 500 reps. I'm sure it even had a cute motivational name like "Friday 500."

I remember thinking then what I always think: "I got this." Over-optimism at its finest.

I got into the workout and quickly realized there was a heavy emphasis on the lower body, which is not my specialty. My specialty is the lay-on-your-back-and-relax segment at the end of the workout. However, at 5'7", I have a built-in advantage—a strong squat-to-distance-traveled ratio—so I figured I could manage.

DISCLAIMER: WHILE THE SQUATS APPEAR TO HAVE INCREASED MY HEAD SIZE, I DO NOT SUPPORT JUICING — METABOLIC OR FRUIT

JELLY-O-METER

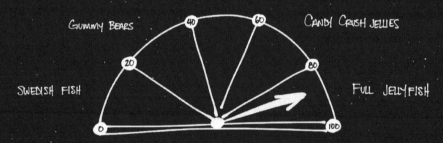

POST WORKOUT
LEG ASSESSMENT

I ended up doing 250 reps of various bodyweight squat exercises during the workout, plus a couple of laps around the building between sets. (Thanks for the "active" rest, Buck.) My legs were wobbly at the end of the workout. "Of course my legs are jelly," I told myself. "I'm supposed to feel worn out after a good workout." Nothing abnormal there. It wasn't until later in the week that I started to suspect a slight muscular malfunction.

I expected to be sore for a couple days, especially after taking that much time off. What I didn't realize was that, 10 days later, I'd still be sore—not to mention that my quads were extremely swollen and inflated to 140 psi from whatever I had done to myself. The cherry on top? My pee was also a little bit brown. (I'm so sorry about that detail, but it's necessary.)

So, I went to the doctor. Keep in mind that it was a week and a half later at this point. I explained what I had done, and the doctor smirked a little and laughed under his breath. I wasn't offended, but rather weirdly consoled by his lack of concern. When we got to the bottom of it, his explanation made sense. He said what I was experiencing was called rhabdomyolysis, "rhabdo" for short. It's caused by the destruction of muscle fibers and release of their contents into the bloodstream.

Destroyed muscle fibers was right! The pee situation suddenly made a bit more sense now—adiós dead muscle fiber. Rhabdo can be serious, but fortunately, it wasn't too serious in my case. It's actually more common with former athletes and military personnel who are more accustomed to pushing themselves mentally—or because they're idiots for thinking they're still as fit as they were when they played high school baseball 20 years ago.

I made an assumption that I could pick back up right where I had left off months earlier. Mentally, I was feeling fully capable and prepared for the workout. My body, however, was having none of that nonsense. What I had actually done was completely over-exerted myself and damaged my quads; I was experiencing a severe case of over-working out.

My doctor gave me a couple of meds to reduce the swelling and basically told me to wait it out. My wife now affectionately refers to the whole experience as the "Fat Thighs" incident.

"Fat thighs" are often a step in the culture-building process, too. If I had been honest with myself and put my ego aside for a minute, I probably would've recognized that 250 squats was not a good re-entry point for me. In fact, I can think of 249 options that would've been a better place to start.

When you're truly self-aware about where you are today—your real starting line—it helps you take the right next step. I could pretend all day long that I was 250-squats material, but the reality was that I was more like 25-squats material that day. Similarly, you can pretend that your communication skills are amazing, that people think you're the best boss in the world, or that you're smarter than everyone else. Maybe it's true, but probably not.

Most of us struggle with being self-aware. We like the idea of being honest with ourselves, but we're usually not completely honest with ourselves. Until we are, we won't make the kind of progress we're hoping for. Our progress will remain unfocused and inefficient.

Don't get me wrong; we will still make progress, but it'll be slow. Even though I did some damage during the Fat Thighs fiasco, I did probably make some small amount of progress when all was said and done. It was just the worst, slowest, most ineffective way to do it.

Be honest about where you're starting today. Being unrealistic only delays progress.

Most of us need a little help figuring out how to do that. So, ask a couple of people you trust for their candid, unfiltered input. Give them permission to tell you what's really happening—and try not to go bonkers when they say something you aren't expecting. After all, you're asking for their help. There's nothing worse than being the only one to think all is well when everyone around you can't believe you don't see the problem for yourself.

What's in it for me?

Choose a group (work, family, team, etc.) where you'd like to see culture change—a new way of life. Identify three to five realities that describe that group today.

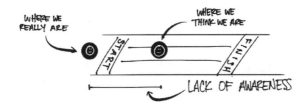

2

FLUSH THAT GOLDFISH ALREADY!

THE CORRELATION BETWEEN YOUR SUCCESS AND HOW QUICKLY YOU RELEASE IDEAS

I'm going to lump everyone who works in a creative industry—graphic designer, filmmaker, copywriter, and so on— into one broad category. We're all *creatives*. Having worked with different creatives over the years, first as a graphic designer myself and eventually as a Creative Director, there is one common quality I've observed in this egotistical field: creatives really like themselves.

A little bit of that attitude is required to be good at the job. I also believe it's a by-product of the work. For example, as a graphic designer, I produced work and clients would give me feedback. If they liked it, I was good; if they didn't like it, I would change it. My work was public for all to see, and its value seemed to be determined by others.

This also makes it easy to wrap up your identity in the work you do rather than basing your identity on the person you are. You want to do work where you have more control—work that paints the right picture of who you are. When do you have the most control? When you're working on your own ideas. This is why creatives seem to love themselves and their ideas so much. It's a defense mechanism. We're protecting our egos.

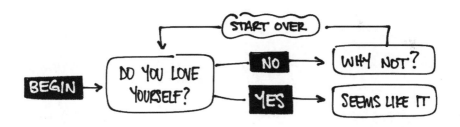

The most successful creatives I know aren't only talented; they also have an uncanny level of humility to handle this ego management. Unfortunately, most of us aren't in this category.

Occasionally, our ideas *are* the best, but usually they're not. It's impossible for one person to always have the best idea. That's not a slight against anybody's competence. It's just basic math: "many" is greater than "one." None of us alone will ever be smarter or more successful than all of us combined.

Here's how this applies to culture, too. There's a direct correlation between how quickly we find success and our ability to release ideas. Usually, the decision to release ideas is about releasing our own ideas. As your attempts to design culture come up short or fail to produce the outcome you're looking for, your ability to consider other options and move on to different ideas will determine how quickly your culture sticks.

Years ago, I was at a conference listening to the CEO of Snapple talk about ideas. He said to treat them like goldfish: When you've got one, drop it in a transparent environment and feed it. If it grows, keep feeding it; if it dies, flush it and get a new one.

During the process of building culture, learn to identify when it's time to move on. And, when it is time, move on quickly. Don't worry about being right; just try to get it right in the end—which might mean going with someone else's idea.

What's in it for me?

How well do you receive and implement suggestions from others? To make sure you're not delusional, think of two to three examples in which you've done this well.

WHERE WE SHOULD RELEASE IDEAS THAT DON'T WORK

WHERE WE END UP FINALLY LETTING GO

LIVE IN THE LGF TIME ZONE "LET GO FAST"

3

POWERED BY PING PONG

CULTURE CAN BE BUILT
ANYWHERE WITH ANYTHING

When I think about culture, I think about ping-pong.

When I worked at Elevation Church, we introduced a Game of the Month, and the level of staff participation in ping-pong suggested this game was in a class by itself. It was more popular than indoor mini tennis, Xbox FIFA tourneys, shuffleboard, office putt-putt, and all the rest. It was here for a month and then gone until next year. (A nice application of "less is more" by Elevation Church game master Josh Blaction.)

One of my favorite memories was watching my friend Jared play.

There was a good chance he was wearing his Newport cigarettes shirt, which had clearly come from Goodwill during his college days at SCAD. The bearded filmmaker was politely sweating and mumbling to himself after chopping a backhand into the net with half the creative department standing around the table in support. On the next point, his hidden athleticism made a guest appearance in the form of a forehand winner, and he smirked just enough to remind us he cared.

Jared was sad. Then he was happy. Frustrated. Delighted. Tense. Annoyed. A full range of emotions in eight minutes while playing with a fancy Stiga paddle in hand and a ping-pong ball we probably bought from Target.

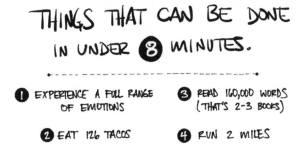

THINGS THAT CAN BE DONE
IN UNDER ⑧ MINUTES.

① EXPERIENCE A FULL RANGE OF EMOTIONS

② EAT 126 TACOS

③ READ 160,000 WORDS (THAT'S 2-3 BOOKS)

④ RUN 2 MILES

It doesn't take much to start creating those culture grooves. Get a paddle—or whatever you have around—be intentional, and you're ready to get started.

What's in it for me?

What opportunities do you have access to today that you could leverage as a culture-building tool? A newsletter? Family dinners? A video camera or phone? Team meetings?

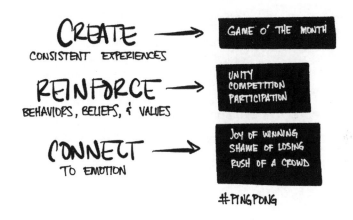

CREATE → GAME O' THE MONTH
CONSISTENT EXPERIENCES

REINFORCE → UNITY
BEHAVIORS, BELIEFS, & VALUES   COMPETITION
PARTICIPATION

CONNECT → JOY OF WINNING
TO EMOTION   SHAME OF LOSING
RUSH OF A CROWD

#PINGPONG

4

GRAB THE LEAF

LEARN WHAT MAKES PEOPLE FEEL LIKE HEROES

I was on a run in my neighborhood earlier this year when I saw a small leaf floating down from a tree. It was doing what leaves do when they fall: twisting around, gliding back and forth, and randomly making its way down to earth.

It was a morning run in late winter. The birds were chirping. No one else was around. I was on a trail that weaves in and out of the trees along a little creek when I saw the leaf. As I got closer to the falling leaf, I reached up, didn't break stride at all, and grabbed it right out of the air.

That's it. That's the whole story.

No one was around. No one saw it. No one even cared that it happened. Except me.

You would've thought I just found out I was a *New York Times* bestseller by the way I felt in the moment. It was only a leaf, but it was also unbelievable . . . to me. I'd never really thought about whether I had deep aspirations to become an accomplished leaf runner. And, regardless of whether this was a big deal to anyone else, I was freaking out inside. I seriously felt like a hero . . . for about 30 seconds.

First of all, I think I was tired from running, so there's that. Second, I never broke stride, and it just felt like something that shouldn't happen, like I was the LeBron of leaf-grabbing. And third, it didn't have to matter to anyone else; it meant something to me, which unleashed the endorphins and emotion for just half a minute.

Becoming aware of what stirs emotion in others will give you a head start on building a better culture. For me, in that moment, it was grabbing a leaf. For your friend Cassie who you meet every

WANTED

HERO
MAKERS

Wednesday for a playdate with your kids, perhaps it's that she feels like a hero when you tell her you think she's a great parent. Or, for one of your employees, maybe highlighting a small victory with a client makes him stand a little taller. For your spouse, saying "thank you" for a clean house may be all it takes.

Acknowledge the small things that make people feel like heroes. If you don't know, ask, and remember what stirs that hero-type emotion in them. Our job as leaders (if you care enough about building culture to read this book, you're definitely a leader; no titles required) is to constantly uncover what activates emotion so we can make sure we're intentionally reinforcing BBV at the right times.

What's in it for me?

Choose someone close to you. What makes them feel like a hero? What makes them feel successful? If you can't answer these questions, pick a starting point and begin the conversation.

5

CASTING CULTURE

THE THREE ROLES FOR CREATING CULTURE

Creating culture requires incorporating three separate responsibilities. This can happen with one person covering all three, or it can be three (or more) individuals who share the responsibilities. However it happens, it always happens.

Each responsibility is associated with one of the following three roles: *Wizards*, *Bakers*, and *Glue Makers*.

Go back to the framework we established earlier and you'll see how each of these roles and their corresponding responsibilities correlate to it:

Create consistent experiences that reinforce behaviors, beliefs, and values, and connect them to emotion.

Wizards

Wizards create consistent experiences that build culture.

This is more than coming up with ideas; it requires the aspiration, authority, or approval to generate ideas *and* bring those ideas to life in the form of experiences. Don't confuse idea people with *Wizards*; they're not always synonymous. In fact, some of the best *Wizards* are people who are great at following through on plans and details — highly organized people.

As an example, *Wizards* are those who plan a going-away party for a friend.

LOOK AT MY HAT! I'M CLEARLY A FANCY WIZARD. HUZZAH!

SOUNDS GOOD, BRO

Bakers

Bakers ensure that experiences are infused with purpose.

They are responsible for making sure that the BBV is baked in. Creating experiences is nice, but creating experiences with intentionality is even better.

That going-away party for a friend is thoughtful, but a going-away party where a few moments are intentionally dedicated to encouraging and affirming the guest of honor before the send-off is better. *Bakers* add this layer of intentionality.

HINT: ITS BREAD

CULTURE LOAF
THE PURPOSE IS BAKED RIGHT IN

Glue Makers

Glue Makers get a return on everyone's effort by making the experience memorable.

Wizards create experiences (throwing a going-away party). Bakers give it purpose (dedicating a few moments to encourage the guest of honor). *Glue Makers* ensure the work of the *Wizard* and *Baker* is effective. They create an experience that matters. *Glue Makers* connect experiences to emotion by finding ways to make the experience memorable.

At this point, everything about our going-away party looks and sounds good on paper, but there's a problem: Plans rarely play out as expected. What if the going-away party is full of introverts who are terrified of public speaking, so what was intended to be an encouraging moment falls boringly flat?

This is where *Glue Makers* make their money. Their responsibility is to understand the dynamics of the room, the people in the room, the flow of the party, and so on. *Glue Makers* are aware of who will be attending the party, understand which guests have the capability to share and encourage sincerely, and have the general wherewithal to visualize a successful party. They ensure the effort matters and is memorable. They make the experience stick.

I'm not suggesting that you write up culture job descriptions for everyone around you (although that might be a fantastic way to reinforce prioritizing culture as a BBV). Instead, I'm highlighting several roles that are always present in the culture-building process. Take any consistent culture experience from your own life and break it down. Who played what role in bringing it to life?

Here's a summary of the roles:

Wizards ask, "What are we doing?"
Bakers ask, "Why are we doing it?"
And *Glue Makers* ask, "How does it make people feel?"

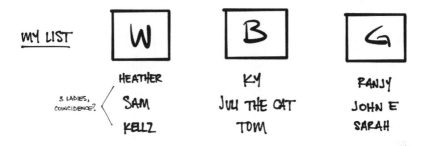

MY LIST

| W | B | G |

3 LADIES, COINCIDENCE?

HEATHER
SAM
KELLZ

KY
JUU THE CAT
TOM

RANJY
JOHN E
SARAH

Ask these questions during your planning process and you'll eventually see a pattern emerge around what sticks with your team, group, or family. When you consistently ask these questions, you're sprinkling in purpose and intentionality. The result will be a smarter process for creating culture.

What's in it for me?

Make a list of the people you currently have around you who fulfill the culture-building roles. Include at least three people in each category— Wizard, Baker, *and* Glue Maker.

SUPPORTING CAST

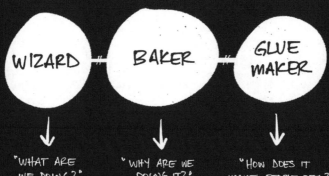

WIZARD — BAKER — GLUE MAKER

↓ "WHAT ARE WE DOING?"

↓ "WHY ARE WE DOING IT?"

↓ "HOW DOES IT MAKE PEOPLE FEEL?"

6

@RYANSWORTH

A little more about *Glue Makers*.

Have you ever heard how glue is made? Originally, it was mostly from horses, which used to be far more common in society because of their transportation and agricultural utility. The protein in the muscle, bone, and tissue of these large, muscular animals was harvested and processed into the earliest forms of glue. Today, glue comes from cattle, pigs, fish bladders (I never really thought about fish having bladders, but kudos to the person who discovered the first fish bladder), vegetables, plants, tree sap, and a variety of other sources.

When building culture, we've established that "glue" is made from

GLUE GUIDE

A BEGINNERS GUIDE TO THE ART OF GLUE MAKING

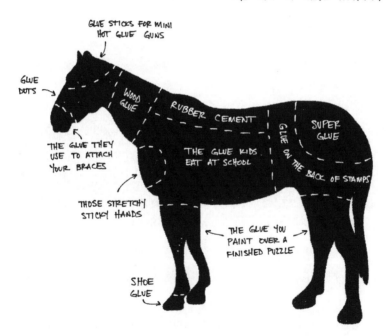

GLUE STICKS FOR MINI HOT GLUE GUNS

GLUE DOTS

WOOD GLUE

RUBBER CEMENT

SUPER GLUE

GLUE ON THE BACK OF STAMPS

THE GLUE THEY USE TO ATTACH YOUR BRACES

THE GLUE KIDS EAT AT SCHOOL

THOSE STRETCHY STICKY HANDS

THE GLUE YOU PAINT OVER A FINISHED PUZZLE

SHOE GLUE

one substance: emotion. Things stick to emotion—positive emotion, negative emotion, short-lived emotion, long-lasting emotion. So, I want to take a couple of pages to recognize one of the best *Glue Makers* I know and describe how he does it:

@ryansworth

(This is Ryan Hollingsworth for those of you who need real names and prefer not to label your friends by their social handles—cutesycol84, sexybible3000, kewlnick4eva, etc.)

Don't forget the framework: Emotion is what locks experiences in. Ryan has the unique ability to create emotion-infused moments for people, and he's a master craftsman at making those moments meaningful.

Ryan's personality is the type that leans heavily toward being creative and embracing his inner performer. He gravitates toward fun and unique experiences, which is why it should come as no surprise that,

10 years ago, he and I entered into a water-drinking competition where we had to drink 20 cups of water a day for five days straight. First one to 100 cups would win.

Why did we do this? Because we're fools. And, because opportunities to create memorable moments are everywhere.

While neither of us actually finished the challenge, I do believe he won. He was drinking filtered water and I was drinking tap water. About halfway through the challenge, my best educated guess is that I had consumed whatever small amounts of bacteria are in tap water at such a high volume that it had an adverse effect on my insides. In Ryan's words, I had the "rumbles." Needless to say, I retired from competitive water-drinking.

1,000 oz + 5 DAYS = BAD IDEA

GLUE MAKERS

MAKE MOMENTS
MATTER

Neither of us cared about consuming that much water for health reasons; we were only interested in the uniqueness of the challenge. Naturally, an element of emotion accompanies uniqueness, and here we are — 10 years later — still talking about it in detail because the details all stuck.

He's a *Glue Maker*.

He's also the one who:

- *Rolled 75 yards down a grassy hill after losing a bet.*
- *Did burpees for a whole mile.*
- *Designed the Nearly 1K Fun Run for our office, complete with a mid-point water station staffed by volunteers.*
- *Started a casual travel and dining club called Meals on Wheels (MOW) that drives to a city for lunch and back in the same day. The catch is that every trip in that calendar year has to be longer than the previous ones — which has the MOW crew traveling for a full day to eat lunch, sometimes hundreds of miles away, by December of each year.*
- *He's the host of the Ellys, the formal annual awards show at Elevation Church, one of the most memorable nights of the year for the entire staff.*

Shall I continue?

- *He releases a popular curated Spotify playlist every season called "Good Medicine."*
- *He once yelled at a friend's grandma for her differing political views.*
- *He ran a marathon with me.*
- *He dressed up as a ninja for one of my kids' birthday parties.*
- *He played the flamboyant role of Chips in the Latino entertainment spectacular Chips and Salsa to entertain kids at camp.*
- *He encouraged me to buy Thinking Robes for our entire creative department just to help spark creativity.*

These are precursors to knee jerks, and I have 100 more examples just like this where he decided to create moments that matter for other people. Ryan has a little bit of all of the roles in his DNA—*Wizard, Baker*, and *Glue Maker*—but he's exceptional at making moments matter.

What a *Jerk*.

What's in it for me?

What are two or three recent examples of experiences that generated an emotion for you personally—positive or negative? What happened? How did you feel?

7

THE SILVERADO CELEBRATION

GRATITUDE IS CULTURE'S CAFFEINE

I can't stand negative people.

My feelings are so strong that I invented a word in response to negativity. Or, at least I thought I did.

I was driving to my office years ago seething over an interaction I'd just had with a friend who is perpetually negative. I was in my green 1995 Chevy Silverado asking myself, "Why can't they have a better attitude? How hard is it to choose to be a little more positive? I wish they would try just a little bit to have a great attitude."

And then, it dawned on me: Great attitude . . . great . . . attitude . . . great . . . attitude . . . gratitude!

I spent the next two minutes celebrating the fact that I had just created a new word—GRATITUDE. It was the best word ever! A combination of "great" and "attitude." It was gratitude!

I was beside myself thinking I had created something new and amazing for the whole world. And then, as fast as the joy had set in, it was gone. "Oh, wait, that's already a word," I realized.

Easy come, easy go.

While I may not have actually created "gratitude," I've certainly seen its effects. Gratitude is a cultural accelerant. It does to developing culture what caffeine does to your teenager. Gratitude increases velocity.

BROTHER + ROMANCE =

BREAKFAST + LUNCH =

COSTUME + PLAY =

CRAZY + DRUNK =

FRIEND + ENEMY =

SPOON + FORK =

When gratitude is flowing, emotion is higher. When emotion is higher, culture is growing.

By this point in the book, you understand the power of emotion. Gratitude evokes a positive sentiment in most people. While it's an unlimited resource, it's also more rare than you may realize. Stop for a minute and think about the interactions you've had this week. How frequently have you seen gratitude on display? Not a cursory "thank you" (even though those can count), but sincere gratitude? I'm betting it wasn't often.

Gratitude is surprisingly absent from our day-to-day lives. This is why we're caught off guard when we meet somebody who expresses gratitude. We don't even know how to describe those people. We end up saying something like, "They are so nice," which isn't even accurate. Gratitude is generally so unfamiliar to us that we even mislabel it.

One of the best teachings I've ever heard on the subject of gratitude was in a sermon delivered my pastor, Pastor Steven Furtick. He preached, "Gratitude is never silent," and it's stuck with me for a decade. People have a lot of grateful thoughts, but very few of those thoughts ever get expressed verbally — or any other way, for that matter. The gratitude within them, unfortunately, remains silent.

Take a moment and ask yourself, "How often do I actually express my gratitude?"

When you do encounter someone who is vocal and active about expressing their gratitude, it presses the emotion button and essentially creates a stickier environment for more BBV to grab hold.

Grateful people are not the primary catalysts for cultural change. But, they certainly expedite the process by creating a more fertile environment for culture to grow.

What's in it for me?

How do you generally express gratitude? Do you assume people already know? Are you better at written expression? Verbal? How frequently do you communicate gratitude?

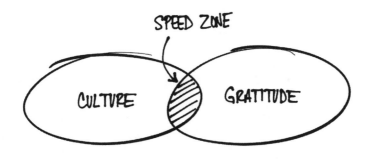

GRATITUDE IS LIKE AN ALWAYS-
ON EMOTION-MAKING MACHINE

8

THE SPEED OF HUGS

GROW FASTER BY CREATING
MANAGEABLE DISCOMFORT

My wife has often accused me of hugging friends too soon. She claims it can be uncomfortable to hug someone before they're ready.

I disagree.

My take on a hug is that it expedites the get-to-know-you process. Even if it can be a little awkward, I like the connection. I think of it as mutually beneficial.

An introductory hug typically prompts one of three responses:

1. You appreciate the hug because it's a friendly gesture.

2. You're caught off guard by the hug, and there's no time to object. You experience quick-onset paralysis for about three seconds.

3. You hate everything about being hugged in general. You endure the discomfort.

Note: This should go without saying, but I feel the need to say it anyway. This chapter is not a license to be a creep. Don't go around randomly hugging people you don't know. And, don't use hugs as a weapon or as a dominant power play. It's a hug; it's supposed to be warm and fuzzy. Don't go around making hugs cold and prickly. Got it, weirdo?

HUG RESPONSES

YOU RESPOND 1 OF 3 WAYS.
AND THEY ALL MAKE YOU FEEL.

"THAT'S NICE"

"I'M PARALYZED, HELP"

"I HATE THIS"

HUG IT OUT

Regardless of the response, all three prompt a feeling. Just like that, the flytrap is open and you have an opportunity to influence whatever happens next. I encourage you to take advantage of the moment and use it to foster a future relationship.

With the teams I lead, I'm usually looking for the culture to be built on friendly, healthy relationships. Consequently, I'm paying attention for moments to reinforce BBV. A hug can create that opportunity, and there are dozens of other actions that can do the same.

I'm not trying to force friendship with anyone who isn't interested. I'm only trying to prime a potential future relationship and set the tone with a hug. When you hug, you're speeding up the process of connecting with someone. That's it.

You may be thinking, "Seriously? All this from a hug?"

Yep.

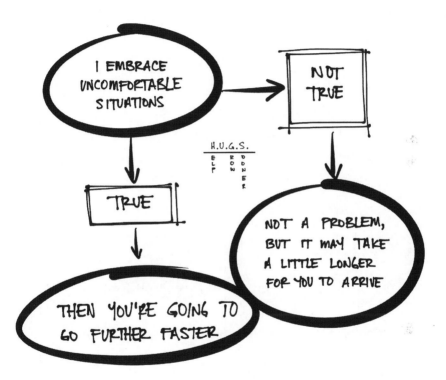

The strongest culture builders understand that creating culture also comes from seemingly insignificant moments, especially the small ones. And, the good news is, if you don't like hugging, don't hug. But do *something*.

What's in it for me?

How do you generally respond to awkward situations? Think of a recent awkward moment. What did you discover about yourself through the experience?

OTHER ACTIVITIES THAT PRODUCE EMOTION

- MEETINGS
- COOKING
- DECORATING
- PERFORMANCE REVIEWS
- BRAINSTORMING
- DATE NIGHT

9

Yours vs Ours

LANGUAGE MATTERS. A LOT.

My family makes it a priority to be involved in our church because we believe our church is making a difference in peoples' lives. Our church can also be a little obnoxious at times, but in a good way. (Is that possible?)

We will correct volunteers who use the word "yours" instead of "ours" when referencing our church—not every volunteer, but some. We're talking about anyone who's been around for a while and has expressed a desire not just to show up on a Sunday, but to be a part of the influence being made through the church. With those people, we're comfortable holding them to a higher standard, because they've "opted in." They want their lives to be meaningful, and they believe church provides that outlet.

But, that doesn't mean that holding them to a higher standard every once in a while when it comes to language isn't also a little annoying.

People often ask, "What's the big deal? Yours? Ours? It's one letter."

But, it's the most important letter, "Y." For most people, "yours" becomes "ours" when they get "why?" When they understand and align with why we do what we do as a church, why it makes a difference in peoples' lives, or why it's important for our personal health, then—and only then—does it become more intuitive and accurate to say "ours."

People will say, "I like what your church is doing" or "You guys are really helping the community." But, "you" and "yours" become "us" and "ours," when you see your involvement at church not just as an obligation or a quota to be met, but something you have ownership in.

YOURS "YOURS"

YOURS BECOMES "OURS"

(Y)OURS ONCE YOU GET "WHY"

For you, it might be work, sports, or a neighborhood group. When people talk about whatever it is as if it's their own—"our team," "we should," "one of us"—it's a small detail indicative of perspective. It reveals a great deal about their motivation, passion, and commitment.

Language is one of the most important indicators of how people really feel. If someone has internalized a belief, they will eventually express it through their words. As you leverage language, the first step is to begin observing it all around you. It'll help you keep a finger on the pulse of your culture.

Addressing language around you to keep it aligned with BBV might feel like an overreaction at times, but that's only until you realize what a powerful tool language is in building culture.

What's in it for me?

What does your language say about your values? What does your language communicate about what's acceptable or unacceptable in your culture?

10

AUSTIN KLEON IS A JERK

PAY ATTENTION TO PEOPLE
SMARTER THAN YOU

I wrote this book because I wanted to read this book. I was encouraged to do so after I read Chapter 3 in Austin Kleon's *Steal Like an Artist*. I loved his book so much—the style, the length, and the message. I also, respectfully, stole his book format for my book. Thanks, Austin!

I like the way he thinks. I like the way he writes. I like that he didn't just have an idea, but he actually brought it to life. When you come across people like this, people who are smarter than you, pay attention. Leadership guru Ken Blanchard says, "None of us is as smart as all of

THINGS SMART PEOPLE DO
(THAT OTHER PEOPLE DON'T DO ENOUGH)

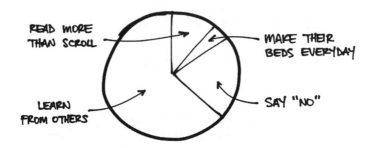

us." That means we ought to put our egos aside for a minute and start learning from others if we want to avoid the lifelong frustration that results from always going at everything alone.

Learning isn't limited by your access to people smarter than you. Most of you keep a screen in your jeans that provides instant access to more wisdom from more people than you can ever process. We all have different reasons to explain why we aren't proactively learning and improving, but access to smart people can't be one of them. We often

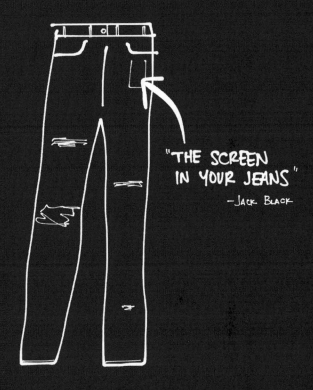

"THE SCREEN IN YOUR JEANS"

—Jack Black

believe it is, but that's just an excuse to make us feel better.

What is true is that I can find someone to teach me:

- How to use a *sous vide* to cook steak (which is now my favorite way to do it)
- Why the little tags on pillows are protected and treated like endangered species
- The difference between a "bop" and a "banger" when my kids are describing new music
- Anything else I'm interested in

And, I can do this with one search in less than two minutes.

As you attempt to establish your culture, start by making a list of people who are doing it well. Here are 10 people from my list—in addition to Austin Kleon—who elicit big knee-jerk reactions from the cultures they've influenced or created. In other words, here's a list of 10 big *Jerks* who are smarter than me and inspire me:

TONY HSIEH zappos
AVA DUVERNAY array
GINGER HARDAGE southwest airlines
PETE CARROLL seattle seahawks
JOHN LASSITER pixar
EMMA CHAMBERLAIN youtube
JOHN LEGERE t mobile
VIRGIL ABLOH louis vuitton
CASS LANGSTON hillsong church
BRENÉ BROWN univ of houston

Regardless of who ends up on your first list, make one. Physically write it down. Study the *Jerks* on your list. Learn from them. Discover how they did it.

What's in it for me?

List three companies, families, or teams who have cultures you admire. Specifically, what do you like about these cultures?

11

4,000 WAYS TO COOK CHICKEN

Do you have any idea how many different recipes I can make if I start with chicken, garlic, onions, and a little olive oil? I searched a popular recipe site with those ingredients and it returned 4,746 results. The majority of the recipes on the first 10 pages of results had amazing reviews.

My point is that there are a lot of different ways — amazing ways — to cook chicken. There are also a lot of different ways to package success. And, there are a lot of different ways to create culture.

Instead of thinking that culture-building has to fit a certain mold or be built on the most original ideas, find a style of culture-building that works for your team. Your process can look however you'd like it to look. Remember, there are more than 4,000 ways that people have enjoyed chicken!

Avoid setting your culture-building standards impossibly high and putting unnecessary pressure on yourself to do what everyone else has done. Instead, learn from others, but set your own standards. Your goal should be to set standards that you find helpful, valuable, or encouraging—not just standards that are identical to everyone else's.

What's in it for me?

Where are you limiting yourself by thinking you've got to build culture a certain way?

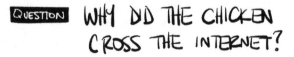

QUESTION WHY DID THE CHICKEN CROSS THE INTERNET?

TO GET TO THE OTHER SITE

12

WHY PEOPLE BUY SNUGGIES

MAKE SURE YOUR MESSAGE
FITS ON A NAPKIN

As I was writing this book, I was struck with the concept for a future book. I think I might title it *Yes, That's True, but I Don't Care*. It's going to address how we deliver accurate facts without actually communicating. We transfer information, but people don't care because we don't provide enough context for why it should matter to them.

In short, we're barely communicating because people don't recognize the value of what we're saying. Yes, they understand the words, but the words themselves have little value to them.

Several years ago, I went through a workshop in Nashville, led by author Donald Miller, called "StoryBrand." In short, it was a course designed to help us clearly communicate so people could understand and respond. I spent three days with a group of 50 people talking about how to communicate more clearly by following the elements of *story*.

One of the points Donald made during that workshop was this:

People will never engage if they don't understand.

Conversely, people will often jump in with both feet when they *do* understand. Case in point, I'm pretty sure no one ever watched an infomercial for a Snuggie thinking, "You know what I could use today? A blanket with arm holes in it that I could wear backwards like a jacket!" But then they watch that infomercial . . .

It starts in black-and-white with a really sad but attractive 28-year-old female looking disgruntled. No matter what she does, her blanket just won't stay on her shoulders. That's when the handsome neighbor

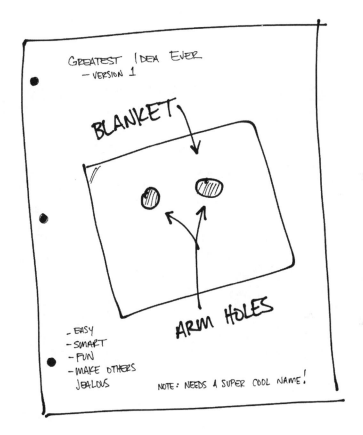

COMPLEX

IS A COMPILATION OF A LOT OF SIMPLE.
BREAK IT DOWN FOR PEOPLE. KEEP IT SIMPLE.

miraculously shows up just in time (why was he able to just walk in the house? Hmmm . . .) and says, "Hey, check out this cool thing I happen to have handy right now!" Life is automatically transformed. The world goes from black-and-white to color and her joy has been restored . . . all because of a Snuggie.

I may not think I need a Snuggie, but I certainly understand what it is and how it appears to make my life better. And, so do the tens of thousands of people who own them today.

So much of our communication style focuses on pleasing *ourselves*. Instead, I encourage you to sacrifice the self-gratification in communication and prioritize clarity and simplicity for *your audience*. The language in this book is intended to be simple enough for anyone to understand. It wasn't written to win a Pulitzer but rather to help people know they can be effective in building culture.

Before passing along instructions, directions, or encouragement to others, ask yourself this question:

Can I communicate this on a napkin?

You don't have a lot of space, so you've got to keep it simple and concise. Can you deliver your message in a couple of sentences? This will give you a better chance of being understood. It will also require more work, but it's worth it. Running communication through this can-I-write-it-on-a-napkin filter will force you to prioritize clarity. It will help people care more about your conversations because they'll be more likely to engage with you.

Bottom line: prioritize clarity over creativity. If you can have both, that's even better, but clarity comes first.

What's in it for me?
Where and how can you simplify your language to prioritize clarity?

CLARITY

— OVER —

CREATIVITY

(IF YOU CAN GET BOTH?)
EVEN BETTER.

13

CAN I GET A $200 CASH ADVANCE?

THE BEST LESSONS LOOK LIKE MISTAKES

It was my freshman year at Pepperdine University. I was trying to find myself, my path, and my new friends, and that made me a perfect target for Carson the Sophomore[1], who lived in my dorm.

I was 17 when I enrolled in college, and there's a lot you don't know at 17. For example, I didn't know that giving someone $200 to buy in to a "business opportunity" by recruiting two others to also buy in at $200 each, and so on and so on, was commonly known as a pyramid

---

[1] I don't remember his actual name, but you'd probably recognize him if you saw him. He was the one walking around with a trail of dollar bills falling out of his pockets.

scheme. I just knew it sounded amazing, and I sounded rich!

"Wait a second. I'm going to give you $200, and in two weeks, you're going to give me $1,600? This is incredible! Why isn't everyone doing this?!"

Because not everyone is a dummy. (FYI, just about every instance in my life that seemed too good to be true . . . was.)

I gave Carson the Sophomore $200 to buy in, already making a mental list of all the things I was going to buy. The very next day, Carson broke the bad news to me, "Sorry, bruh. Things didn't work out. Deal's off." I was bummed, but at least I'd get my money back.

"Sorry, dude. You're not getting your money back."

"That's impossible," I thought. "I took out a cash advance on a credit card to get in on this sure thing. I have to get my money back."

No dice. My money was gone.

If you could draw a *Highlights* magazine "What's Wrong With This Picture?" of this entire scenario, you would circle about 16 different things, but I didn't see any of them. Probably because I didn't want to see any of them.

As you're building a culture, you're going to have ideas that you believe are bulletproof. You'll believe this because you don't know enough to confirm whether this is actually true. Other times, you'll believe your ideas are right because you believe you're smarter than everyone else.

Either way, test your ideas if you feel strongly about them.

Just know that you're going to get it wrong sometimes. When you do, the temporary shame and embarrassment you feel will make sure you never forget the decision you made, and you'll know better next time. This is why life's best lessons often look like mistakes.

Acknowledge what happened, learn, and move on. After all, it's only a temporary setback. You'll be alright—a little smarter, and only out $200.

What's in it for me?

Identify a culture-building idea you have right now. Bounce it off two to three people you trust to give honest feedback on how they feel about it.

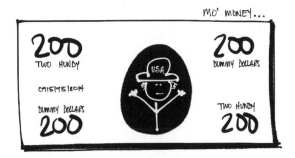

"THAT'S RIGHT, YOU GIVE ME THAT $200 DOLLAR BILL, AND I'LL GIVE YOU A $1,600 DOLLAR BILL NEXT WEEK"

14

SUPER 77

THERE ARE NO SHORTCUTS

I had this idea to fix my oldest daughter by the time she turned 13.

As an opinionated son-of-a-tiger-mom with some mild control issues, this seemed reasonable to me at the time.

My original plan was to create an experience where I could do some course-correcting as my oldest daughter was about to hit her teenage years. My intentions were pure: "She's about to enter one of the most formative periods of her life. Why not help her fix all of her problems and chart the course for the rest of her life at 12 years old?"

The plan was simple: Take the 90 days before she turned 13 and spend time with her every day. We were going to be intentional about spending time together, just the two of us. Maybe five minutes, maybe an hour. It didn't matter; we just had to be together every day.

You may have noticed that the name of this chapter is actually "Super 77," not "Super 90." About that . . . I was supposed to start 90 days before her birthday, but I miscalculated and missed the 90-day mark. The next best option was 77 days because "Super 77" has a nice ring to it. And, just like that, a well-branded 77-day experience to change my daughter's life began.

Without going into all of the detail, fast-forward 77 days and we did it. We met (just about) every day for 77 days. We missed a couple, but downgrading one more time to "Super 75" is really embarrassing, so I don't talk about that. I captured everything we talked about, where we met, and the progress I felt we were making. I've got four girls, and I was laying the foundation to do this three more times.

Here's what I learned:

ALTERNATES

- ~~NINETY DAYS OF POWER~~
- ~~AWESOME NINE OH~~
- 3 ~~MONTHY~~ SCHMONTHY
- ~~FAMILY FIXIN' TIME~~
- ~~NIFTY 90~~
- ~~NIFTY 77~~
- ~~77 GOIN' TO HEAVEN~~
- SUPER 77

I should stop trying to change people.

You'd think this would be a little more intuitive for me. It wasn't. We become so myopic when we think we have all the right answers.

When I finally stepped back, I was reminded that my oldest daughter was already amazing. No fixing required. No need to accelerate the growing up process, even if my intentions were to help.

As much as I didn't want to admit it then—and still don't like to admit now—there are no shortcuts. I thought I had master-planned the process of growing up, avoiding mistakes, and doing everything right. I thought, "Just follow me!" I was wrong.

If you can look past my dysfunction for a minute, there actually was a benefit to Super 77, but it wasn't what I thought it would be. It was the consistent time we spent together. That's it.

Throughout that 77-day window, we developed an ability to

communicate more thoughtfully. We discovered what we really meant when we said certain things. We learned how to recognize each other's body language better. We decided how to deal with each other when we were annoyed or bored or disinterested. The fact that we made an effort to get together regularly was great for our relationship.

Stop trying to shortcut growth because you're being impatient. Remind yourself that growth comes from the process along the way, not just from results.

What's in it for me?

What shortcuts are you trying to take to expedite your culture growth? What are you hoping to avoid by taking a shortcut?

LIGHTS WILL GUIDE YOU HOME
AND IGNITE YOUR BONES
AND I WILL TRY ... TO FIX YOU

WHAT WE THINK
ABOUT A SHORTCUT

START ●————————————————————● FINISH

(ACTUAL ROUTE)

WHAT REALLY HAPPENS
USING A SHORTCUT

START ●

FINISH

(ACTUAL ROUTE)

15

I DON'T MIND BEING WRONG (BUT I'M NOT)

CULTURE IS STRONGEST WHEN WE EMBRACE OUR DIFFERENCES

I used to think everyone hated being corrected. Then, I discovered it's not everyone; it's me who doesn't like being corrected. Or being told what to do. Or feeling like I'm incapable. Or not in control. And, it makes me feel good to assume *everyone* or *most people* or even *a lot of people* are just like me.

Maybe they are. They're probably not. Either way, my focus is wrong. I'm too focused on comparison whereas I should be asking myself, "How can I embrace someone who is different than me?"

I read a *Harvard Business Review* article a few years ago on the topic of "business chemistry." I was obsessed with it for the next six months. It gave me words for something I had believed for years but hadn't known how to articulate.

It suggested that the best leaders understand how to embrace people's differences, and, consequently, they're the ones who get to harness the full power of collaboration.

Culture develops faster when you quit thinking a bunch of people just like you would make everything better. A bunch of people like you would only make everything boring. Learn to believe "different" isn't just okay, it's necessary and better. Differences are what enable you to solve problems in a smarter, cheaper, faster, better way.

Allow people to challenge the way you think without creating unnecessary tension by being defensive. I love tension. I love to argue. Unfortunately, I do it too much and often just for the sake of it. Consequently, I miss opportunities.

BEING RIGHT

— VS —

BEING BETTER

Take a cue from the brain trust at Pixar. They've created a feedback process that allows peers to speak into each other's work on a regular basis. They're not trying to win when critiquing one another's work. They're only trying to illuminate weak points in the plot so the director can improve the story. They've discovered how to release their egos enough to constructively receive feedback from other people.

Follow the lead of the Pixar directors who recognize the value in different perspectives. For them, different perspectives mean better stories. For us, different perspectives can mean better cultures.

Quit trying to be right. Start working toward embracing "different."

What's in it for me?

Describe the main differences between you and those around you. Where are you stronger than others? Where are they stronger than you?

16

I VERY DON'T LIKE YOU

FAILURE IS THE FASTEST EMOTION

Some writers write and it's obvious they were meant to write—
Stephen King, J.K. Rowling, Anne Lamott. I fall into the category
I describe as "functionally ambitious." I've got more passion than
ability. My technique isn't polished. I'm comfortable with the thought
that my writing won't be the best; I just want it to be helpful.

I like to think my writing career started in Olympia, Washington, at
Capital High School back in the '90s. I took an AP English class my
senior year. I was going for college credit after a counselor came in
and gave us a pitch about taking AP classes to get a head start on
college. Sounded good. Complete the course, take the final exam, and
score a 4 or higher to qualify for college credit.

I got a 3.

Nonetheless, I still learned a lot about writing that semester. But, I never learned more than I did from a two-second interaction with one of my classmates, Leah. She was one of two students in my graduating class of 300 with perfect grades—all As, all four years. But, she wasn't the highly academic, no-interpersonal-skills type. She was actually pretty great . . . until the day she pantsed me with vocab.

We did a lot of peer evaluation because our teacher was smart and knew that utilizing free public school student labor is a lot better than grading 30 papers every night and missing *Family Matters* re-runs. Leah was my partner and she was giving me feedback on a writing sample. The entire exchange literally took two seconds, but I'll never forget her feedback.

She read my work, looked up, and said, "'Very' is the tool of a weak mind." That's it.

What?! I don't even know if I actually understood what she meant. But, I understood enough. "You are not a good writer."

I didn't know it then, but I know it now: Failure fosters unforgettable memories. Failure is why I still remember the word I missed when I was eliminated from the fourth-grade spelling bee: H-O-N-O-R-A-R-Y. No wonder the fear of failure is widely considered one of our greatest fears. Failure is so hard to shake. Even when we've moved past its emotional effect, we have a hard time forgetting it.

I'm not advocating failure as the emotion of choice for establishing culture. However, I am challenging you to recognize that failure is as sticky as any emotion. The associations around our failures stick with us. Be mindful of the experiences you attach to failure in the culture-building process.

Failure is a healthy aspect of growth. As leaders, we like to say, "It's okay to fail." If that's true, we have to make certain that our people connect beneficial memories and experiences to failure. When an employee misses a deadline, loses a sale, or simply makes a poor decision, the conversations that follow can be the difference between a culture of growth and safety or a culture of fear and shame.

What's in it for me?

What is your most recent failure? What is your first failure you can remember?

17

SWEATY-PALMS CONVERSATIONS

GOOD CULTURE REQUIRES
HEALTHY CORRECTION

If you aren't willing to initiate uncomfortable conversations every once in a while, you have no chance of building a thriving culture. Good culture requires healthy correction.

Name the last difficult, corrective conversation you had with someone. One where you were correcting a decision or a behavior—or one where you were being corrected. Correction causes that pit in your stomach. When you know it's coming, your palms get sweaty. Just the anticipation leading up to the conversation can feel unbearable. But, if you're trying to reinforce BBV, correction is one of the most helpful tools you have.

Unfortunately, correction is too often assumed to be negative or hurtful. And, while it can be, it doesn't have to be. Correcting your kids so they don't play with fire is good. Correcting a friend because you think they have bad fashion sense, well, that may fall more into the negative/hurtful category. Yes, it may be true; they may be terrible at assembling a publicly presentable look, but *correction* and *opinion* are not the same.

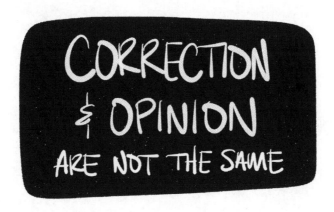

CORRECTION vs CULTURE

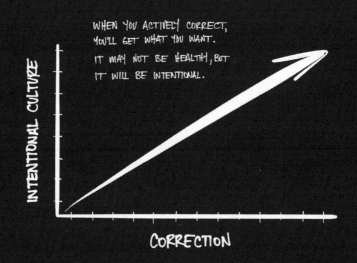

WHEN YOU ACTIVELY CORRECT,
YOU'LL GET WHAT YOU WANT.
IT MAY NOT BE HEALTHY, BUT
IT WILL BE INTENTIONAL.

INTENTIONAL CULTURE

CORRECTION

Opinions can be great to have. Share them with others if you've got enough in the relational account to cover the potential withdrawal. Opinions can be great for your relationships, but they serve a very (thanks, Leah, I know, my mind is weak) different purpose than correction.

Correction, when done well, moves people toward a desired outcome. It shouldn't highlight a deficiency and foster shame. In other words, healthy correction is helpful.

"Helpful" doesn't imply it won't sting a little bit. I can't think of one person I know who enjoys being corrected. My immediate response to correction is often to get defensive or find a way to reframe the conversation. I often have to remind myself that correction is healthy when given and received with the right perspective and motivation.

You affect culture when you bring attention to issues that influence BBV. And this requires you to initiate a few sweaty-palms conversations every once in a while.

Dr. Martin Luther King Jr. once said, "It's always the right time to do the right thing." Apply that thought to our conversation and it might read, "The right time to have the right conversation is right now." I believe your culture depends on it.

What's in it for me?

When was the last time you initiated a sweaty-palms conversation? What was the outcome?

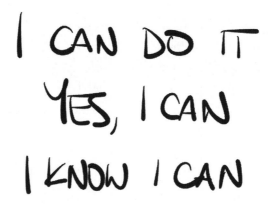

18

VALEDICTORIAN SCHMALEDICTORIAN

EMPATHY IS THE MOST HELPFUL TOOL
FOR WORKING WITH PEOPLE

There's a fantastic book by Daniel Goleman that came out in the 1990s called *Emotional Intelligence*. It speaks to how empathy may be more important than intelligence in helping people become successful. In a more recent podcast, he shared an interesting example of an informal survey he performed with hundreds of CEOs. When he asked how many of them had been valedictorians, only a couple raised their hands. Daniel's point was that superior intellect isn't a prerequisite for success; rather, success is more frequently correlated to a person's ability to understand how to work with other people.

Moreover, I believe empathy—knowing what language people understand and recognizing how people feel—is the greatest tool for relational success.

Empathy fosters better culture. Because culture is shaped by how people think and behave, your ability to relate to and understand people affects the speed at which knee jerks become the norm and culture is established. Think of empathy like fertilizer for a garden. It's not entirely necessary, but it facilitates the growing process.

But, being empathetic doesn't mean you're always concerned with everyone's feelings. It's more about recognizing how people perceive, feel, and want to respond.

For example, I can feel nervous that you may not like a constructive comment I made about your work without being empathetic. Empathy would express itself more along the lines of, "I understand how much time went into this project, but because we're up against a tight deadline, I need to be more direct than usual with my feedback."

What's in it for me?

How well do you recognize people's feelings? Give an example of how recognizing someone's feelings helped your response to a particular situation.

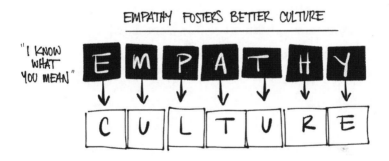

19

PINKY PANTS

DON'T TAKE YOURSELF TOO SERIOUSLY

If you've read anything from Brené Brown, you've certainly recognized her uncanny abilities to understand how people think and to dissect what's really motivating their behavior. In her bestseller *Daring Greatly*, her research and explanation of how shame affects us will change your life.

One of my major takeaways from the book was to learn to laugh at yourself and not take yourself so seriously all the time. That's my translation.

Years ago, I was headed to an event with several people from my office. Five of us jumped into the car of one of my coworkers. That meant three people in the backseat. I was in the backseat on the right side, next to a female friend—let's call her Lolly.

As we were leaving, I went to put on my seatbelt. You know how sometimes the person in the middle will be sitting on the buckle? It can be a little tight, and you have to somehow figure out how to get to your buckle; that's what I was dealing with. Lolly politely leaned to the left so I could grab the buckle. I went to click in my seatbelt, and then . . .

. . . the pinky on my left hand inadvertently slid right inside the edge of Lolly's denim pants! It was obvious skin-on-skin contact with her bare upper-outer hip. I quickly pulled my hand back and looked directly at her. Clearly, we were both fully aware of what had just happened.

All I could say was, "Sorry about that." I was mortified.

I hope Brené would be proud of me because my embarrassment quickly turned to humility and I just started laughing. No hiding from the moment. It was obvious it wasn't intentional, and we moved on. Thank God she was a good friend who could laugh it off, too. It was one of those moments that could be extremely awkward if you let it get the best of you.

Can you imagine what it would it would've been like if we hadn't laughed? The last thing I want to do is carry around unnecessary angst all day from a split-second experience that means absolutely nothing in any of our lives. It was an innocent mistake.

You will have many awkward moments in the process of fostering transformation with your team. But, fortunately, your ability not to take yourself too seriously and laugh off some of the awkward times will be one of your greatest defenses against feeling like you're constantly carrying the weight of performance and perfection on your shoulders. Of course, there are certain matters that will require your attention. You can't always use laughter as an excuse not to address issues. Address important matters, but filter out the smaller stuff that easily entangles your mind and infuses shame. Learn to laugh a little

HOW TO CREATE AWKWARD

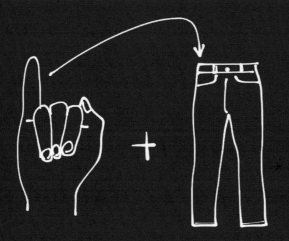

more and move on.

What's in it for me?

*Describe a recent situation where you wish you would've laughed it off
instead of letting it get to you. Why didn't you?*

HOW WOULD YOU RESPOND?

— GET CRAZY **OR** STAY CALM —

YOUR TEACHER ANNOUNCED
A BAD SCORE YOU
RECEIVED OUT LOUD

YOUR SHIRT WAS ON
BACKWARDS AND A
CO-WORKER POINTED
IT OUT

YOU WERE FIRED
FROM A JOB

YOUR CHILD WAS
SUSPENDED FROM SCHOOL

20

PRAY YOU NEVER WIN THE LOTTERY

———————

WE LIVE AND DIE IN TRANSITIONS

Imagine a set of stairs. The tread of each step is 10 feet long. This is a model of how most of our time is spent. We live life on a fairly even plane, we encounter an obstacle, and we level up. When we level up, hopefully we get a little smarter and carry that wisdom forward onto the next plane.

The step up initiates transition. And we live and die in transitions.

The large majority of life is spent walking across these long planes. I don't know what the percentage is, but let's assume the Pareto principle (the 80/20 rule). It states that in all events, 80% of effects

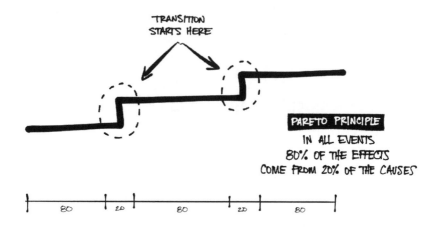

come from 20% of the causes. This implies that 80% of our lives are dictated by 20% of our decisions. In other words, 80% of our lives are determined by how we handle the transitions that follow our decisions.

The majority of the time, you stay the course, learn to develop routines and habits, and remain as consistent as possible. Then, you experience the occasional opportunity to step up—a defining moment, even if it's a small one. Following the step up, your focus should change to managing the new level you're on—managing the step and life after the step. How will you handle living on a new level? This is the transition.

The step up usually includes a deeper insight, an increase in resources, or a fresh perspective. It's not always positive or easy, but it's always an opportunity to grow.

Although it's not always a financial step up, let's use this as an example. If I get a raise at work, how I allow the raise to affect my future makes a difference. If I choose to respond by upgrading from a Mazda to a Mercedes, that decision may have a significant influence on my perspective, my attitude, or my relationships. And, how my perspective, attitude, or relationships are affected is the essence of living and dying in transitions.

I'm not anti-driving-a-nice-car, but I am anti-not-having-an-awareness-of-how-transitions-affect-you.

This is the reason why so many lottery winners go broke. Research shows that lottery winners are significantly more likely to go bankrupt than the average person—and it's usually within five years of winning! The problem is that they don't know how to manage the transitions; they step up, but they don't manage life well after the step.

While culture begins to take hold around you, the way that you personally handle the transition of new, better, or different will affect how people around you embrace the change themselves. The answer to how we best handle transition is different for all of us. But, it starts in the same place for everyone—a heightened awareness that the period after every step up is where we're most susceptible to failure.

What's in it for me?

Describe how you generally handle transition. Do you embrace change? How does it make you feel? How quickly does this happen?

21

AM I THE ONLY ONE SEEING THIS?

EXPECTATION ARE BETTER
WHEN THEY'RE SHARED

It wasn't too long after moving to North Carolina from the Pacific Northwest that my wife Kelly and I attended our first Southern wedding. We headed to Charleston, South Carolina. The wedding was at the Magnolia Plantation. Picturesque, humid, charming—everything you'd expect from a Southern summer wedding.

Kelly and I drove onto the property and immediately came across some debris in the middle of the road. As we approached—and unless that was a prehistoric log with legs—we were watching an alligator cross the road!

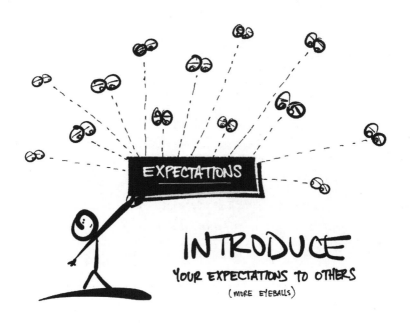

INTRODUCE
YOUR EXPECTATIONS TO OTHERS
(MORE EYEBALLS)

I looked at Kelly completely dumbfounded, wondering if anyone else was seeing this right now—an alligator casually crossing the road?! This NEVER happened where I grew up. I've lived a lot of places—both coasts, overseas, Las Vegas—but none where certain death walked in front of your car on your way to a wedding.

After telling friends at the wedding, I experienced the greatest of letdowns. What I hoped would be a flurry of inquiries like "Are you okay?" or "How did you get away?" turned into nothing more than dismissive responses like "Cool" and "Yeah, we saw that, too." What was wrong with them?

Expectations unmet. Super unmet.

Apparently, alligators were already a familiar sight to almost everyone else at the wedding because they had grown up in the South, where alligators roam the streets freely with no curfew. I had been hoping for a more validating response. Isn't that what we're always wanting—someone to validate our perspective?

We are masters of passive-aggressive finger-pointing. We're not going to say it's your fault. But, inside, we'll blame the frustration from our unmet, uncommunicated expectations on other people. We'll assume they should know what we're thinking just because we're thinking it. Why do we do this? Because we don't like being at fault.

Here's an easy solution:

Share your expectations.

You don't have to go above and beyond; just communicate the basics when you have the opportunity. You'll arrive at your destination more smoothly when everyone knows where you're going. For example, when you share with the team that your goal is for every tenured team member to initiate a weekly conversation with every first-year team member, it's far more likely to happen just from that small expectation being set.

People are designed to work toward a goal or destination. People also like helping other people accomplish their goals. Sharing expectations with others will always increase the likelihood of them coming to pass.

What's in it for me?

What expectations do you have for the culture you hope to build? Who needs to know those expectations?

EXPECTATIONS
HOW WOULD YOU LIKE THEM?

☑ EXCEEDED
☐ MET
☐ IGNORED
☐ UNMET
☐ SUPER UNMET

22

DON'T MAKE ME SEND YOU TO VOICEMAIL

BUILD CULTURE WITH PEOPLE YOU LIKE

I have a personal philosophy on hiring: I won't hire anyone I don't like. I know it sounds pretentious, but why would I? Talent only gets you so far, and talent is a lot easier to find than a good culture fit. If I am going to build anything worth being a part of, I'd like it to be with people I enjoy being around. I'm going to get down in the trenches and live my day-to-day with them, so the last thing I'm looking for is someone I want to send to voicemail every time their name pops up on my caller ID.

You may not be in a position to hire, but you are in a position to surround yourself with specific people. Again, I'm not condoning a

HIRING CHECKLIST

☑ COMMUNICATION SKILLS

☑ COMPETENT

☑ CULTURE FIT

☑ REFERENCES

☐ DO I LIKE THIS PERSON?

judgmental disposition or an exclusive attitude. I'm simply suggesting that culture is built by people, so if you have any influence on which people are part of your culture, you should exercise your influence.

It makes more sense to enjoy the process of getting where you're going if you have some control, even a little. There's no need to unnecessarily act like a martyr and suffer for no reason.
Control what you can control. Influence what you can influence.

In the words of Miranda Priestly, "That's all."

What's in it for me?

Which people in your life drain you and which people energize you?

"HI, THIS IS LARRY. JUST HANG UP AND TEXT ME."

DID YOU KNOW?

18% OF ALL VOICEMAILS ARE DELETED BEFORE THEY'RE LISTENED TO

— THE INTERNET

23

CARROT OR STICK

KNOW WHAT MAKES YOU GO

One of my favorite books of all time is *The Ragamuffin Gospel* by Brennan Manning. One line from that book hit me the minute I read it, and it has been with me since I was 18. He wrote, "People would rather be drawn by love than chased by fear." I couldn't agree more.

Let's play it out. If you gave me a task to move a horse from here to there (which is probably a pretty common task for Gen Z kids these days), there are many ways to accomplish that. I could just grab the reins and start pulling, and if the horse is in a good mood, I might get lucky. But, if the horse is still cranky from all the glue-used-to-be-made-from-horses talk, I could be in for a fight. Either way, I'm hoping for the best, but I'm also prepared to muscle through it,

if necessary.

The problem with this approach is that it's too unpredictable. It also relies too much on my own strength, and maybe on a little bit of luck, too. An alternative is to acknowledge that the horse is already pretty good at moving itself. If I can motivate the horse to move in the direction I want it to go, I'll be much better off.

If I were the horse, I'd definitely have a preference for how I'd like you to motivate me. I'd like to be drawn forward by something enticing, like a nice baby carrot. That would do it. However, I also don't enjoy being swatted with a stick, so that would motivate me pretty well, too. The fear of that momentary sting is definitely enough to get me going.

So, which is it, the carrot or the stick? The reality is that both motivations—the carrot and the stick—move the horse. According to Brennan Manning, however, we all have a preference and would much rather be drawn by that carrot.

Whether you choose the carrot or the stick may be a matter of asking, "What's my best option *right now*?" Or, maybe you need to ask, "What's my best option *long-term*?" The stick is usually more immediately effective, but it may not create the best dynamic over time between you and Starlord (that's your horse).

In one of my past management roles, I asked my team what I could do to motivate them better in the future. At the top of the list was more money or more time off. Following those were public recognition and

increased status or influence. Everyone's preference was the carrot. But, I have an idea that if I'd told everyone the next project deadline was job-dependent, the team would've been as motivated as ever.

Cultures based on fear—on sticks—can be productive. However, study any cult or dictatorship ever, and you'll find fear-based cultures are rarely healthy. Fear-based cultures often prevent teamwork, hinder good communication, and destroy confidence.

As the leader, it's my prerogative to motivate however I want to motivate. I just have to recognize that, while effective, a fear-based style of motivation may not be as helpful in keeping the team together or healthy over time. Both motivation styles—carrots and sticks— move people and create culture. It's just that one tends to be more desirable and sustainable.

What's in it for me?

Make a list of three to five people, places, emotions, experiences, or aspirations you find motivating.

GRASSHOPPERS

ESTABLISH TRADITION TO RALLY AROUND

The most challenging part of creating culture is being consistent. Essentially, just about anyone can make their performance spike above the "exceptional" threshold one or twice. Real *Jerks* have figured out how to consistently maintain that exceptional performance above the threshold.

To foster consistency, create traditions that prompt culture-making behavior.

While coaching my youngest daughter's under-eight, coed, rec-league soccer team (that just felt like a Starbucks drink order), I knew we weren't going to win a bunch of games. My experience playing soccer was limited to some PlayStation FIFA all-nighters in college and the one year I played when I was five years old and living in South Korea.

So, I recruited my friend Jamie, who actually played soccer in college, to coach with me. Jamie was going to provide the skills training, and I was going to do what I do: find a way to create a memorable soccer experience—and it wasn't going to include a whole lot of soccer. Instead, it included stars to put on your jersey for "player of the game," bribery for accomplishing in-game tasks ("Who wants ice cream? Great, I want to see 20 passes this game!"), and "Chariots of Fire" playing on a tiny speaker in the background during our pre-game pep talks.

Best of all was our team's rally cry. It was a declaration! This was the culture-making tradition every player and parent knew we were going to belligerently shout in unison before we took the field for every game. Imagine this call and response between the coaches and 10 seven- and eight-year-olds:

Coaches: HOW DO WE PLAY?

Kids: HARD!

Coaches: HOW DO WE WORK?

Kids: TOGETHER!

Coaches: NEVER GIVE UP!

Kids: NEVER SURRENDER!

Everyone: GOOOOOOO GRASSHOPPERS!

Yes, we were the Grasshoppers. That's the name the kids chose, and I owned it like my life depended on it.

But, that little pre-game ritual accomplished a few things:

1. It created energy through anticipation. Our players looked forward to yelling at the top of their lungs and making a spectacle of themselves.
2. It intimidated opposing teams. We had a mental edge as the game started because it's not too hard to intimidate other eight-year-olds. (That edge dissipated, of course, about two minutes into the game because no amount of hype can cover up a legitimate lack of talent.)
3. It created a rallying point. It checked our boxes: consistency, reinforcing team values (work ethic, unity, perseverance), and creating emotion to secure the memory.

This is how culture is built. We participated in traditions while reinforcing BBV. The result was a greater level of energy, effort, and performance from our team. Consistently.

Create traditions to rally around. The Grasshoppers are proof it works.

What's in it for me?

What specific values do you want to reinforce within your group?
Describe a tradition you'd like to create that would help reinforce these
values?

PLACE YOUR BETS

ACCORDING TO SURVEYS, WHAT ARE THE **4**
MOST POPULAR SPORTS TEAMS
NAMED AFTER ANIMALS?

#1 CHICAGO
BULLS

#2 PITTSBURGH
PENGUINS

#3 ST LOUIS
CARDINALS

#4 SEATTLE
SEAHAWKS

2/2/14 ⟶ 43-8

25

I'M A SUCKER FOR MARKETING

YOU BETTER LOVE IT IF YOU
WANT ME TO LIKE IT

Have you ever heard this quote? "Shoot for the moon. Even if you miss, you'll land among the stars." That's by Norman Vincent Peale, author of *The Power of Positive Thinking*. For most of us, that sounds more like the makings of a meme or an inspirational poster gone bad. But, he's right.

We don't normally change our behavior overnight, or our beliefs, and certainly not our values. Consequently, we have to place a premium on the process of how we transfer culture.

I'm a serious sucker for marketing. I joke all the time about how I'm constantly victimized by a good infomercial. In college, I bought an "As Seen on TV" product for $300. It was a speed-reading course. It had a 30-day money-back guarantee, so I bought it knowing I would send it back. (Hold your judgment please; I already told you, I was a broke college kid back then taking all kinds of unsuccessful shortcuts).

The course taught you to overload your brain and senses. It was designed to force you to process information at abnormally high speeds, so when you went back to reading at a normal speed, your brain was processing faster. And, that meant speedier reading. Made sense to me.

At one point as I was going through the exercises, I had the book flipped upside down and I was turning the pages as fast as I possibly could, swiping each page top-to-bottom with my finger. I would stand up and sit back down every few seconds, and I would wiggle my toes the entire time. Yes, it was everything you're imagining.

But, when you train yourself to do that every day for a few weeks, you'd be shocked at how much information you can take in over a short period of time when reading normally. In other words, on a scale from 1 to 10, let's say I read at a level 3 speed to start. During my training, I was cranking the information overload up to a 10. When I finally went back to reading normally, it felt like I was reading at a level 5 or 6 speed. It worked!

And I still sent it back. (C'mon, I could go grocery shopping for six months in college with $300 — ramen, spaghetti, frozen burritos, day-old bread, off-brand peanut butter, Totino's Pizza Rolls, etc.)

When transferring BBV to others, you need to overdo it to ensure you're making progress. If you're reinforcing BBV with 9 out of 10 intensity, it is likely to transfer to others at closer to a 6 or 7.

Set high standards for language. Challenge values in a way that feels impossible at times. Set a pace for your team that leaves you out of breath. At the same time, being selective where you want to overdo

HOW CULTURE SPREADS

ALWAYS BURNS HOTTEST AT THE START

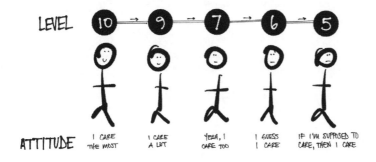

LEVEL	10 →	9 →	7 →	6 →	5
ATTITUDE	I CARE THE MOST	I CARE A LOT	YEAH, I CARE TOO	I GUESS I CARE	IF I'M SUPPOSED TO CARE, THEN I CARE

PASSION FADES DOWN THE LINE

it—and implementing those selections in moderation (don't try to do everything at once)—will help you make progress toward new BBV.

What's in it for me?

Give an example of something you're passionate about that others would say you often overdo. Is it your intensity in conversation? Your attention to detail or being organized? How you throw parties? This may be a good behavior or value to start with when building culture.

BECAUSE BEHAVIORS,
BELIEFS, AND VALUES
DON'T CHANGE OVERNIGHT,
YOU HAVE TO PLACE A
PREMIUM ON THE PROCESS
WHEN CREATING CULTURE,

26

THE RHYTHM METHOD

START WITH PEOPLE'S NATURAL
PATTERNS AND PREFERENCES

In a past job, I was part of a team considering new software to help connect people online. We would give people a chance to build an online profile, post pictures, leave messages and comments for one another, and provide updates on their daily activities.

Stop for a minute. I'd like you to think about what I just described for a few seconds. When you hear that description, what comes to mind? What existing online community-building platform do you think of?

You got it; they made a movie about it. We love to hate it, but we all have accounts. Facebook has more than two billion registered users. That's more than one quarter of all the people on the planet. Seems to be working okay.

That platform that Mark Zuckerberg created was a good idea. The one we launched wasn't.

At the time, we felt confident that we could create a customized tool that was going to provide people with a valuable experience. We rolled it out, and we let it run its course for several months.

Do I even need to finish the story?

There's no drama here. This is the worst suspense story ever told. It didn't work. Almost no one liked using the tool consistently. We invested, tested, and then quickly abandoned the whole idea.

Think of it this way. When I open my laptop, I always have a browser open already. Inside that browser, I have about eight tabs that are also already open. One is my email and one is a calendar. I've also got a couple sites I visit to read articles, and a couple of social networks. I

IF EVERYONE HAS A PATH THEY'RE ALREADY TAKING, DON'T MAKE IT HARDER TO SELL YOUR SPANISH LEMONADE BY CHANGING THEIR BEHAVIOR. GO WHERE THEY ALREADY ARE!

LIMONADA

25¢

DON'T MAKE IT HARDER THAN IT HAS TO BE

keep *The Seattle Times* open because I like the local guys talking about the local teams, and I even have one tab open that curates daily deals on the web. I've got eight that I already visit every single day.

Why would I want to add another one?

But this is exactly what we were attempting to do. We didn't recognize that we were essentially asking people to change their behavior by adding another tab to their daily online routine. People don't want to add more to their lives. If anything, they're trying to make life simpler.

We missed a fundamental principle: to successfully enhance someone's quality of life with a new service or tool, you should begin by acknowledging the paths they're already walking on—and assimilate into those paths.

You never want to leave people where they are, but you do want to start by meeting them where they are.

When trying to reinforce BBV, introduce new standards, habits, and traditions by integrating them into your team's current routines and daily flow. Doing so is a lot easier than trying to change their behavior all at once.

Brain science tells us we process familiarity much faster than unknown factors. According to Harvard professor Dr. Srini Pillay, unfamiliarity increases stress, and stress makes us less "friendly" toward our situations or circumstances.

People change when *they* want to change, not because we think they should or because we have such incredible ideas and opportunities for them. Our opportunity for culture change is to be a part of the consideration set when people are ready for change. If we're already integrated into their routines, we have a greater chance of positively affecting change.

What's in it for me?

Identify where you may be asking people to step outside their natural routines or patterns. How can you meet them where they're at?

UNOFFENDABLE

BE HARD TO OFFEND

I want to be hard to offend.

I've marketed several bestselling books over the years. My favorite project to work on was written by my pastor, a book titled *Crash the Chatterbox*. The Chatterbox represents that voice inside all of us that is incessantly trying to foster fear, shame, discouragement, and anxiety.

One quote from the book reads, "The voice you believe will determine the future you experience." It reminds me of the importance of not only developing thick skin but also being selective about whom I listen to. I'm not condoning suppressing your emotions and never feeling anything. I'm only encouraging you not to allow your inner critic or feelings to have the final say on your future.

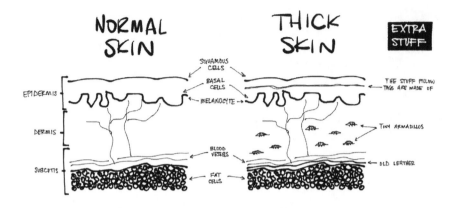

NORMAL SKIN

THICK SKIN

EXTRA STUFF

SQUAMOUS CELLS

BASAL CELLS

THE STUFF SKIN TAGS ARE MADE OF

EPIDERMIS

MELANOCYTE

DERMIS

TINY ARMADILLOS

BLOOD VESSELS

OLD LEATHER

SUBCUTIS

FAT CELLS

When we introduce new BBV—or anything new for that matter—we subject ourselves to the responses and opinions of everyone involved. Change will evoke feelings. Processing those feelings in a mature manner involves learning how to filter them by taking what's helpful and leaving what's unproductive. Filtering well is the best defense against offense. Being hard to offend isn't a prerequisite for culture; it's more of a supplement to improve the process.

Remember, being offended is a choice, which also means that not being offended is a choice.

What's in it for me?

Choosing from these two options, how would you describe yourself: hard to offend or easy to offend? Explain.

28

WHEN WE HAD KIDS, WE...

BEGINNINGS ARE ALWAYS AWKWARD

When Kelly and I started having kids, we got a lot of advice from everyone:

- *If one of your kids throws a tantrum, throw a bigger one.*
- *Don't leave Legos on the floor.*
- *Choose your battles.*

And, my favorite…

- *When your baby is teething, rub a little whiskey on her gums to soothe her.*

No matter what advice we were given or which books we read,

parenting was impossible to fully prepare for. We simply had to go through the process ourselves. No amount of prep could truly prepare us for being parents; we just had to become parents.

The awkwardness of initiating cultural change can be similar.

For example, if one of the new behaviors you'd like to implement is publicly affirming employees more often, this will be awkward at first. It's a wonderful practice and you know the framework, but when it's not a way of life already, it's going to be awkward.

Imagine this scenario: You have six people on your team. You are the leader and you decide you'd like to reinforce affirmation as a value. Your hope is to slowly move your team culture toward consistent affirmation. One day, you pull everyone together for your regular team meeting where you typically cover stats or provide project updates. Then, before you wrap up, you stop and say, "Today, I'd like to do something a little different. I want to take a moment and recognize Zelda"— clearly, she's got millennial parents—"for something

THE REALITY OF STARTING

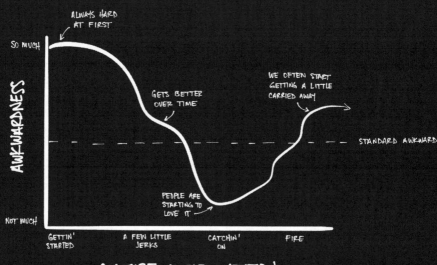

ALWAYS HARD AT FIRST

GETS BETTER OVER TIME

WE OFTEN START GETTING A LITTLE CARRIED AWAY

STANDARD AWKWARD

PEOPLE ARE STARTING TO LOVE IT

SO MUCH

NOT MUCH

AWKWARDNESS

GETTIN' STARTED

A FEW LITTLE JERKS

CATCHIN' ON

FIRE

CULTURE IMPLEMENTATION

she's done."

Let's pause and break down what's happening.

We should be aware that, at this moment, the team is curious, a little nervous, and possibly even confused about what's going to happen. They understand what you said, and they're wondering why you said it. It's new to them and, remember, people generally don't know how to initially handle the unknown. Consequently, everyone in the room feels a little awkward.

Fortunately, empathy is your ally when it comes to building culture. You have to recognize what people are thinking and feeling to best help them.

Until your audience becomes comfortable with this new routine, the awkwardness won't go away. That's because atmosphere is generally created by audience response, not by the person on stage or up in front. Parents know this; it's the reason they start clapping and cheering as if everything's okay when their 2-year-old takes a tumble. If their response indicates that everything is okay, the child will also think everything is okay. Audience response dictates atmosphere.

If your audience responds in just the way you hope—excitement, enthusiasm, engagement—great! But, let's face it: most beginnings are awkward, so be prepared. It can take time to change an audience's response.

The team in our imaginary scenario may need a month or two of consistent affirmations at team meetings for the process to become familiar and for them to get comfortable. When they do, the awkwardness will dissipate and, through sincere affirmations, these exercises during team meetings will become one of the most anticipated moments of the week—in a good way.

EMPATHY IS YOUR ALLY

What's in it for me?

Awkwardness makes most of us uncomfortable. On a scale from 1 to 10—with 1 meaning you will do whatever it takes to avoid speaking of the awkwardness ever again and 10 meaning you comfortably push through the awkwardness—how do you respond to awkward situations?

PAIN MEASUREMENTS

STEPPING ON A CLOUD	STEPPING ON A CORNDOG	STEPPING ON FIRE ANTS	STEPPING ON FIERY COALS	STEPPING ON LEGOS
0	25	50	75	100

29

GIVE ME AN EXAMPLE

SPECIFIC EXAMPLES OF HOW CULTURE CAN BE BUILT

When you write a book like this, everyone wants an answer to one question: "What's the best way to do it?"

I don't know.

There is no best way to do it. There are only different ways to do it (like cooking chicken). This book was never intended to be a tool for building a specific type of culture; rather, it was intended to help you understand how to build the culture you want, as opposed to telling you what kind of culture is best for you.

With that in mind, here is a series of examples and commentary based on our culture framework. They illustrate how certain behaviors can translate into knee-jerk responses. Your job is to translate how these examples apply to you.

TRANSLATION PLEASE

CULTURA
SPANISH

CULTUUR
DUTCH

MO'OMEHEU
HAWAIIAN

문화
KOREAN

文化
CHINESE

MORSE CODE

EXAMPLES

NO SET OFFICE HOURS

FAMILY DINNER CONVERSATIONS

FREE EMPLOYEE SNACKS

WEEKLY CHORES LIST

VOLUNTEERING WITH FRIENDS

EMPLOYEE O' THE MONTH

CORRECTING BEHAVIOR OR ATTITUDE

NO SET OFFICE HOURS

Create consistent experiences...

Flexible office hours are in place every day. It couldn't be more consistent.

...that reinforce behaviors, beliefs, and values...

This is an example of how something consistent can be easy to take for granted. Reinforcing a particular value requires intentionality. If the value is to trust your team by not micromanaging their schedules, one option is to reinforce this value in a monthly meeting by making mention of it. Or, by highlighting a success story related to strong schedule management.

...and connect them to emotion.

Success stories generate emotion; that's one option. Fear also creates emotion, and this is a second option. The threat of having to move away from relaxed office hours can make the conversation memorable, resulting in the reinforcement of your positive value—I trust you.

FAMILY DINNER CONVERSATIONS

Create consistent experiences...

These don't happen naturally. They have to be initiated regularly. Once a week is a realistic frequency to start for most families.

...that reinforce behaviors, beliefs, and values...

The nature of this behavior reinforces the values of communication, unity, and interactivity within your family.

...and connect them to emotion.

If you initiate the conversation, plan to ask a question that requires thought and can't be answered with a rote response. For example, ask something that evokes emotion: What was the best part of your day? How was that test you were studying so hard for? If you could travel anywhere in the world, where would you go?

FREE SNACKS FOR EMPLOYEES

Create consistent experiences...

Make them available regularly. This may not mean all the time, but consistently—on Mondays, after 4 p.m., before 10 a.m., after a goal is met, to kick off a project, etc.

...that reinforce behaviors, beliefs, and values...

Place a sign next to the snacks that says, "Thank you for working hard." This is an example of how a simple gesture reinforces a behavior and a value. Conversely, you would create a culture—albeit a negative one—if your sign read, "For being so lazy, you've earned these snacks. I hope they give you more energy to work harder."

...and connect them to emotion.

A "thank you" is powerful. However, it may not always generate the same level of emotional response over time. So, changing the note next to the snacks is a small adjustment to keep the emotion fresh and flowing. Remember, gratitude accelerates the adoption of any culture.

WEEKLY CHORES

Create consistent experiences...
It's weekly. That's consistency.

...that reinforce behaviors, beliefs, and values...
Chores, by nature, reinforce BBV. Similar to working out, they provide
repetition that promotes BBV.

...and connect them to emotion.
The emotion can come from the prospect of getting a reward—
an allowance, for example. It can also come from the fear of
consequences associated with not completing chores—such as being
grounded.

Note: 12-year-olds aren't thinking about how much they can't wait to do chores. But, culture is not about whether they develop an affinity for chores. Culture is a way of life.

If the byproduct of weekly chores is that your 12-year-old knows they need to be done weekly and actually does them, that's culture! If your hope is for your 12-year-old to do them with a great attitude (gratitude!), that's a different behavior or value to reinforce altogether.

VOLUNTEERING WITH FRIENDS

Create consistent experiences...
Establish a cadence—once a week, month, or quarter.

...that reinforce behaviors, beliefs, and values...
The group members may have different motivations. One person may enjoy the company of friends, one may love to serve the community, and another has FOMO and doesn't want to miss out again after seeing everyone post on social media last month. Individuals may have their own unique motivations, and your job as the leader is to develop an awareness of what motivates each individual.

...and connect them to emotion.
Afterward, ask everyone to share what they enjoyed about the experience. This type of ask amongst friends is, unfortunately, more unusual than common today. But, at some point, someone has to break the pattern and work through the awkwardness if a better culture is your goal.

EMPLOYEE of THE MONTH

Create consistent experiences...
Monthly is the consistent expectation.

...that reinforce behaviors, beliefs, and values...
Regardless of what the employee is recognized for, values will be reinforced. Commonly, Employee of the Month is associated with some sort of best performance. Make a point to explain why the monthly award is being given out—hitting monthly sales goals, the individual with the best time management, the team member most welcoming of visitors, whoever went above and beyond their job description, and so on.

...and connect them to emotion.
Receiving an award or being publicly recognized are two strong tactics to evoke a positive emotion. Do you remember any awards you've been given? I still remember getting an award for a poster contest sponsored by a local fire department in second grade!

CORRECTING BEHAVIOR OR ATTITUDE

Create consistent experiences...

Commit to consistency in order to avoid sporadic correction. Random isn't sticky, and inconsistent won't help a culture take hold. It'll be viewed more as a one-off correction.

...that reinforce behaviors, beliefs, and values...

Correction naturally reinforces BBV by aligning understanding. The individual being corrected may not agree with the correction, but correction should provide greater clarity.

...and connect them to emotion.

Rewards and consequences prompt emotion. If an employee has a bad attitude about having to finish a last-minute project, address it. If a child has a bad attitude about how a particular teacher called them out in class, address it. These consistent conversations, infused with reward and/or consequence, will provide enough the emotion to begin integrating a particular attitude into your culture.

Note: I don't intend to sound like correcting behaviors or attitudes is easy. This is basically the million-dollar question behind parenting and leadership. It's a massive conversation with thousands of books already written on the topic.

Instead, my intent is to highlight the fact that culture can be built to include a specific attitude or outlook as a way of life. For example, highly successful organizational leaders generally have a belief or attitude that they will be successful. This belief informs their culture because misaligned perspectives and attitudes are addressed. BBV is established as a result.

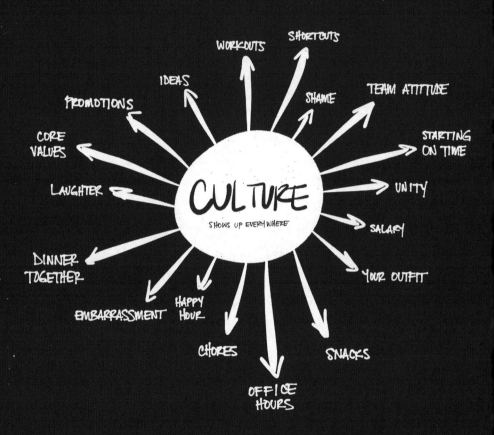

30

NEXT STEPS

WHERE DO YOU GO FROM HERE?

In closing, I'd like to offer an honest word of encouragement: This is an imperfect process, and you're not alone in the frustration you're going to encounter.

Okay, so it's kind of back-handed encouragement, but it's still a good reminder.

If you have a sibling, you have certainly had an experience at some point in life where you were wincing, shoulders tense, eyes half-closed, waiting for them to punch you in the arm. For me, I was always being punched as retaliation for something I had done first—and my sister was five years older and could punch like Piston Honda.

That feeling of waiting—the anticipation right before the punch—was the worst part. It was never the punch itself. Sure, it never felt good getting hit in the arm, but that pain always wore off quickly. In reality, that moment where you were just waiting was the payback.

The waiting and worrying that comes along with anticipating that punch, just like anticipating whether your efforts to create culture will stick, is the worst part. In this case, the punch is the failures that inevitably come with trying something new. You know the punch is coming—we've covered that—so, tell yourself it won't feel that bad and the sting will wear off.

The culture-building process is messy. It can really deplete your reserves when you feel like it's not working. It didn't turn out exactly how you were planning. So, what? Yes, you're a little worn out, and maybe you've got fewer resources than you had when you started. If that's as bad as it gets, you're doing all right.

The biggest *Jerks* I know aren't necessarily the strongest people, but they are the ones who realize trying and failing is a necessary stop on the road trip to figuring it out. Take a deep breath; try to relax a little bit. Yes, the punch is coming, but it's never as bad as you think it will be. You've got this. And, now you're ready to go build the culture you've always wanted, you little *Jerk*.

EPILOGUE

It's 6:44 a.m. on Sunday morning. My family is going through the weekly ritual of trying to get out of the house on time for church. Kelly and I are up first, getting ready, warming up with a cup of coffee (only Kelly though, I'm not much for coffee . . . which makes me a disgrace to the Pacific Northwest), walking the dogs, and making sure everyone is up.

The goal is to be out of the house by 8 a.m., but it rarely happens. We're usually within about five minutes, but still not successful in getting all six of us out on time. The 18-minute car ride isn't bad most weeks. People are still waking up. The blood is just starting to flow through the veins of our four teenage girls, who would certainly prefer a p.m. start time for church.

I'm surfing satellite radio trying to find a bop to set the tone for our commute. The playlist management in the car isn't a democratic process, so I make the choice: "Bizarre Love Triangle" from New

Order on the '80s on 8 channel. One daughter shouts out, "I love this song!" The rest couldn't care less. They're more interested in refreshing their social media platforms to see what their friends have been doing in the 15 minutes since we left our house.

We get to church, and everyone's starting to chatter a bit. They're all finally getting going. The girls are volunteering in the baby rooms and helping with the elementary kids. Kelly and I are saying our hellos and working our way around to catch up with the volunteer leaders in our Care Team roles.

We all settle in, enjoy an encouraging and hopeful morning at church, and head home energized around lunchtime. We're talking through what we learned because everyone in the car knows I'm going to ask, "What did you learn today?" Sometimes, the answers are insightful. Other times, they sound more like fulfilling an obligation so they can get back to *Toon Blast* and "likes."

Either way, the whole morning is a reflection of the family culture we've created. It's our way of life every Sunday morning.

From the cup of coffee my caffeine-addict wife asks me to brew for her a few minutes before we walk out to the car to the follow-up conversation on the drive home, it's all a part of our family flow. It happens consistently every week. We're mindful about reinforcing what our family stands for, and my role as Chief Culture Creator is to make sure there's enough variety to make the moments continue to matter.

Every person who reads this book should consider this an introduction to creating culture. The process will take time. But, if you stay the course and remain intentional about what you're building, it won't be long before you get that small glimpse of hope. It'll be in the form of a reflex. It'll be subconscious. And it'll be all the motivation you need to feel like you're on your way.

Throw on those culture pants and get after it. Good luck!

ABOUT THE AUTHOR

Larry Hubatka is a General Manager for the Marketing and Creative Agency, Tiny Horse. He has provided more than 20 years of creative and strategic leadership for many of the largest companies, nonprofits, and ministries in America. His interests include 90s rock, the Seattle Seahawks, art, family roadtrips, and Jesus. Larry, his wife Kelly, and their 4 girls live in Charlotte, NC.

ACKNOWLEDGEMENTS & THANK YOUS

Jesus
Thank you for the life I get to live, the people I get to live it with, and the opportunities I'm free to pursue. I'm doing my best to give you all of my life in return.

My Wife
The culture we've built in our home is one of my greatest feats as a husband and dad. Thank you for making this book possible by being right by my side the whole way. Loves.

Riley, Lily, Audrey, and Lucy
We would have no culture in our house without all of you. You are the reason our family is the way it is. Thanks for making our marriage full and fun, and for being the kind of daughters every dad dreams of having. This is a sweet note; please remember it and make sure you take care of Mom and me when we're old and slow.

Nick and Heather Dooley
You are our best friends, and best friends come in handy when you're tackling new things. You helped us more than you know with your conversation, encouragement, and friendship. #fcm

Ranjy Thomas
Thank you for all the phone calls and visits during the last 25 years that helped me develop my perspective.

Ryan Chahgingsworth
I had fun winning (and losing) alongside you for the last decade. You are the ultimate memory machine. I hope to be more like you one day. Except for when it comes to the things I don't like about you.

The rest of the Popdogs
Long live the Bad News Bears of church creative. It was the honor of a lifetime leading you and learning from you. You are the characters that gave my own story so much color. Break!

The couple that rented us that RV years ago to drive to NYC
Not sure why you trusted us or if it was even legal to have that many people in the RV, but you sparked a culture revolution.

Austin Kleon
Really love your books. They inspired me to become an author. Thank you.

Brennan Manning
The Ragamuffin Gospel changed the way I see life. Thank you.

Lynn Vincent
Thanks for the encouragement to get this book across the finish line.

Kyle Young
Thank you for giving me a new stable to call home. The way you navigate the world inspires me.

The Tiny Horses
You are the team that makes what we do worth doing. Thank you for being smarter than me in the things you do. You energize me and challenge me to be a better leader.

Chubbs, Yoshi, and Wayne
Loved changing the world together. Suite 33 forever.

Buck Buhler
Thank you for using fitness to abuse my body for many years.

Jamie Waldron
You are the most memorable coach who's ever coached. Thanks, friend. Never give up . . .

Tony Robbins
I appreciate you for flipping my worldview upside down in my first year out of college.

OTHER RANDOM STUFF I LIKE

WEBSITES

SEATTLETIMES.COM
DEALNEWS.COM
ISSUU.COM

PEOPLE ON IG

KOOKSLAMS
HOUSE OF HIGHLIGHTS
PAUL NICKLEN
BLAKE.242

MUSICIANS

LEON BRIDGES
SAINT MOTEL
INDIE POP PLAYLIST (SPOTIFY)
SHE & HIM

BRANDS

PORTLAND GEAR
FEETURES SOCKS

FAQs

Why did you write this book?

Same reason I ran a marathon…I just wanted to do it. I liked the challenge of doing something new and difficult. After 40 years, I've discovered I like new things. This was new. I liked it enough to do it again, but we'll see how this goes first.

Favorite food?

Hands down, Korean food. Rice, kimchi, bulgogi.

Ever played MASH?

Yep. Lived in a shack, married the pink Power Ranger, honeymooned in a dumpster, and had 14 children. I'd say I nailed that one.

Do you think kids should have cell phones?

When they're ready. It's never been about an age for our family. It's more about when kids are ready. "How do you know when they're ready?" is what always comes next. Same way you know when they're ready to date, get a job, or move out… you don't. You make the best decision you know to make, and if it's wrong, you try again. It's a lot like the goldfish. Our kids ended up getting phones with limited app access around 13. That worked for us. I think. Check back when they're 40.

Do you have any pets?

Two Siberian huskies – Dubs and Rocket.

OTHER RESOURCES

If you enjoyed this introduction to building a better culture, pick up the companion workbook that walks you through a 30-day, step-by-step practical process to building your specific culture. Or, sign up for a You Little Jerk Culture Workshop. It's an interactive discussion with other aspiring *Jerks* just like you—people who are passionate about creating a better future.

Find these additional resources and more at:

youlittlejerk.com
culturepants.com

SOCIAL SECURITY & PIN NUMBERS

If you're the kind of person to hide money in your mattress or keep a spreadsheet with all your passwords, this page is for you. I've provided this page for all your most secret personal information. Who would ever suspect you'd keep all that information right here!

SOCIAL SECURITY NUMBER:

DEBIT CARD PIN:

NEIGHBOR'S GARAGE CODE:

TINDER LOGIN:

CULTURE
IS COMING

Made in the USA
Columbia, SC
07 January 2020